It's Not About Donkeys and Elephants
Branding the Real Enemy

By
StressFreeBill

Medsabi Publishing

Medsabi Publishing
Medsabi LLC
Celina, TX

ISBN: 9781521976975

For those family members that sacrificed for our country with their support, service, and blood...

I remember.

Table of Contents

FORWARD

I'm known online as StressFreeBill for a combination of reasons. One is that I used to own a business marketing stress mitigation products to Medical Doctors. Another reason has to do with a weird set of circumstances that caused me to start an online presence in the early days of social media. In 2009, businesses were crashing left and right (including one that I had owned for 20 years). I didn't commit suicide or bury my head in the sand after almost losing everything, so when someone online jokingly called me by that name, it stuck.

If anyone really has some inexplicable desire to know more about me I've tried to include the salient points of my life in the *About the Author* section at the back of this book. What is relevant to our discussion here is that I consider myself fairly normal. I grew up without a father but never gave it a second thought because I had a very loving mother and grandparents. We didn't have any money but I never felt poor. I mostly paid my own way through three and one-half years of college until I impatiently left to start my first business. I've travelled the world rather extensively since I became an adult but have always called Kansas, Oklahoma, Texas, Missouri, or Arkansas home. I've had money and I've wished I had money...

All of this is to say that I consider myself a fairly well grounded average individual that loves his family and proves it by working hard every day. If I have one redeeming above average quality it is probably my tendency to pay attention to the things that interest me.

One of those things that interest me very much is politics. Another is my country. For whatever reason, I grew up to be a very patriotic person.

This is the point where most authors would give you a list of impressive credentials. They would humbly mention their several degrees in economics and political science, cite their years of government service, or casually mention the different news programs where they have served as a guest panelist. They would try to impress upon your subconscious, *Listen to me, I'm an expert.*

I don't have any of that.

What I do have is several decades of watching Washington go about the people's business. I've paid attention, done a lot of research, and reached what I believe are some very fundamental realizations about how our country actually works – and amazingly, no one seems to talk much about it. Most talking heads spend their time focusing on battles between Republicans and Democrats, or Conservatives vs Liberals (or Alt Left, Alt Right, etc.). And because of that, most Americans are used to thinking about politics in these same terms.

I've come to believe that politicians, the mainstream media, and the rest of the east and west coast *powers that be* are simply too close to the trees to see the forest. In other words, they are so caught up in the same old political games that many of them simply cannot see what is really going on. Many others *can* see clearly, but they desperately hope *you* don't…

Here is what I see…

A new **Ruling Class** has emerged in America. And they could care less about donkeys and elephants.

How do I know this? Because *Behavior Never Lies...* and the behavior of these disparate groups no longer makes any sense under our traditional system.

Normally, StressFreeBill would smile at the antics in Washington and laughingly suggest that it's never made any sense... *But this is different.*

The current forces behind American politics play their manipulation games and leave the rest of us to fight it out over the things they really don't care about. The less we know about how things really work, the better it is for them.

A new **Ruling Class** *has* emerged in America and it's about time we started talking about it - and doing something about it. It didn't happen overnight, but they have only recently been brazen enough to expose themselves fully – *they are that confident of their hold on power...*

Whether you consider yourself Republican or Democrat, whether you are a Never Trumper or voted for our President, Bernie Sanders, or Hillary Clinton, you should be concerned about this... *it threatens our very freedom.*

Make no mistake, you will find no conspiracy theories here. Only documented facts and cited references that will expose the way things really are. As a matter of fact, I have a simple request of you... Don't believe what you read here because I say it's true; believe it because once it's been pointed out you can see it for yourself. Indeed, *thinking for yourself* is a disappearing critical skill that is also threatening our freedom and future.

Be warned... StressFreeBill pulls no punches. The simple truths shared here may cause you to question some beliefs you've carried your entire life. But if you follow the evidence, and think it through logically, you may find yourself looking at politics differently - and it may start making way too much sense.

I'm sharing these observations and conclusions because I love the United States of America and I want to see her remain free and strong. I also have some suggestions on how *We the People* can fight back. I suspect that others share my concerns, but unlike many of the professional politicians and pundits, I claim to speak for no one but myself. But I feel compelled to speak... and I thank you for listening.

StressFreeBill
www.StressFreeBill.com

CHAPTER ONE

StressFreeBill is On a Mission

I'm going to do something that isn't considered to be very smart. I'm going to start this book by giving you my *Call to Action*...

I should know better. I've become a professional author and have had some modest success. This is actually my seventh book, but the first in the non-fiction category. The other six are in the science fiction genre and have actually done quite well. They are written under my other pen name, William Lee Gordon, and can be found on Amazon (if anyone is interested).

Anyway, the typical formula for a book of this type is to make your case and build up to the big conclusion at the end. Hopefully, readers will be so convinced and inspired by then as to be totally receptive to the author's *Call to Action* that closes the book.

The thing is, I'm not trying to impress any critics. If you read the Forward you know this book is a work of passion and carries a message that, I believe, the American people need to hear. So, I am giving you my conclusion and my Call to Action up front in the hope that you will stick around and read the rest to let me prove my case. In a hopefully entertaining way I believe I can thoroughly convince you that my conclusions are correct and my solutions are valid. At the very least I believe I can leave you warned and on the lookout for further evidence.

I have already given you my Conclusion: **A new Ruling Class has emerged in America.**

Now, here is my Call to Action... We must immediately stop referring to the *Powers That Be* as the Establishment and the Mainstream Media (You cannot defeat an enemy unless you can correctly name them). We must brand them for what they have truly become: **The Ruling Class** and **The Ruling Class Media.**

That's it. Pretty simple, right?

Of course, selected parts of the media are only one faction of a number of disparate groups that make up the new self-appointed Ruling Class, but we need to draw special attention to them. And there are certainly other things we need to do to take our government back - and we will discuss all of the groups and all of the things. But, why is simply branding the hypocritical elements of our mainstream media the all-important first step?

You'll need to keep reading to find out (pretend you can see me smiling).

CHAPTER TWO

You Can't Win the Fight If You Can't Even Name Your Enemy

We've all grown up thinking that politics is about the battle between Republicans and Democrats. We might use different words like conservative and liberal, or Left vs Right, or whatever...

But we have all been indoctrinated to think of each other in terms of quarreling family members – we may have differing ideas, but we're all Americans.

Because the vast majority of Americans still think this way, politics has become incomprehensible to us – current events make no sense.

How can any leader justify University Presidents ordering the police to stand down while violent protesters (rioters) hurt people, light fires, and smash windows to *shut down* free speech?[1] Liberals used to be on the other side of this issue - what happened?

How is it that members of a President's own party opposed and actively campaigned against him?[2] The 'Trump Wave' has brought more voters and election victories to the Republican party than they've experienced in decades. Yet, many well-known Republicans still openly oppose him, while others silently stand back and do little to help or defend him. Why?

How did we get to a place where the Democrat party can rig a Presidential Primary for a certain candidate, get caught, and still get away with it?[3]

How is it that Republicans control the House, the Senate, and the Presidency yet still can't prevent popular legislation from being slow-walked - if not stalled altogether?

If the Republicans control the government, why has a Special Counsel been appointed to investigate what *everyone in Washington DC* knows to be bogus and exaggerated claims of Russian influence and collusion in our elections? Yet the felonies *we know* were committed (involving Hillary's email, the Clinton Foundation, and the leaking to the press of Classified and Privileged Information) go uninvestigated?

To most Americans, it feels like the whole country has gone crazy.

And while that may have some truth to it, there is a method to the madness...

StressFreeBill would like to share some simple truths with you – a level of understanding and insight seldom discussed on radio and television, and never in the mainstream press. This is not wild speculation, just basic facts that lead to undeniable conclusions.

The first simple truth we're going to look at is easy. It's easy because it's a Truism.

Here is the first simple truth:

You can't listen to what they say; you have to focus on what they do... because *Behavior Never Lies*.

So many of us get sidetracked because we spend an incredible amount of time trying to figure out if the person we're listening to is being honest. StressFreeBill would suggest that we're focusing on the wrong thing.

Let's take the example of Congress...

Everyone is frustrated with Congress. Their approval numbers are at rock bottom and everyone talks about gridlock in Washington.[4] *We the People* vow massive turnover come election time – yet the incumbents are returned to office in overwhelming numbers.[5] What's going on?

Yes, most people are frustrated with Congress, but at election time they listen to their Representative explain about the difficult and Byzantine rules for passing legislation and determine (because they believe him or her to be sincere) that it must be the other Congressmen causing the problems.[6][7]

Leaving aside for the moment that the Byzantine rules are mostly fraudulent (designed to give the politicians cover) and the fact we're choosing to believe professional politicians (no comment needed), *what does being sincere have to do with anything?*

Whether my Congressman is a manipulating lying sack of sand or a naive patriot that is being manipulated, whether my Senator has an elitist attitude and could care less about the *Will of the People* or is an honest person that just isn't strong enough or competent enough to stay the course... *What difference does it make?*

When it comes to the people destroying our country it doesn't matter whether someone is a manipulator or the manipulated, following them will lead to disaster. And make no mistake; our politicians are leading us to disaster. In this book, StressFreeBill will show what behavior to look for in our politicians to know which (few) are the good guys.

Another quick example in the mainstream media would be George Stephanopoulos, Chief Anchor and the Chief Political Correspondent for ABC News. He used to work in the Clinton White House and has donated to the Clinton Foundation.[8] [9] [10] He can claim to be an impartial journalist, but he should be judged based upon his actions; and his actions demonstrate a sickening level of bias.

Behavior Never Lies.

Now that we can agree on *how* to look at things, let's talk about *what* to look at...

The first thing to realize is that our current way of looking at things no longer applies.

Most of us are still using an old, outdated paradigm. You may be challenged to accept the new reality; accepting the unknown is always scary. You may be tempted to throw away the ideas in this book as wild… but there are no conspiracy theories here – just logical conclusions drawn from cold hard facts.

And once you've had a little time to start viewing the media, politicians, university professors and the like through the lens of these simple truths you will quickly realize that *We The People* are being manipulated.

Here is the second simple truth:

The political battle lines in our country are no longer drawn as Republican vs Democrat – it's now about the self-appointed *Ruling Class* vs *We the People*.

At first glance, this might seem contra-intuitive. After all, we are told the rhetoric and hate being thrown back and forth by the Left and the Right are at an all-time high in nastiness and dishonesty.

Actually, this isn't true.[11] In the election of 1800, for example, Thomas Jefferson's camp, among other things, accused President John Quincy Adams of being a hermaphrodite (publicly and in print).[12]

But remember: Regardless of what they say, we need to look at the underlying behavior. *Don't focus on the trees; look at the forest.*

Yes, liberals and conservatives have their differences, but all this divisiveness serves to distract us from the real (and far greater) power struggle being waged in America...

There are certain professions and organizations that institutionally believe they are better than you. They believe they are smarter than you and they believe they better know what's best for everyone. This belief in superiority is so ingrained that it supersedes traditional morality and ethics. Indeed, in many cases, it gives them the justification to ignore laws and violate the US Constitution.[13] In their mind, the ends justify the means and there is too much at stake to leave everything in the hands of *'The Masses.'*

This self-appointed **Ruling Class** consists of these groups (which will be discussed at length in the following chapters):

- The Ruling Class Media
- Ruling Class Politicians
- The Ruling Class Bureaucracy
- The Ruling Class Intelligentsia
- The Ruling Class Oligarchs
- The Ruling Class Judiciary
- Ruling Class Suck-ups

Like in any war, many of the frontline soldiers have simply been manipulated to believe certain things. So, while not everyone in the above professions are philosophically aligned with the Ruling Class, many have been unwittingly drafted into the groupthink. It doesn't make them bad people... it just makes them tools being used by those that are.

The self-appointed Ruling Class doesn't hold meetings, elect officers, or have a secret handshake... but they do have a unifying purpose.

Here is the third simple truth:

The unifying force behind the self-appointed Ruling Class is the doctrine of Globalism.

Globalism is not a new concept. Alexander the Great wanted to unite the world under his rule and actually came somewhat close. Conquering dictators like Hitler have always had similar ambitions.

It can be argued, however, that it was the communists and socialists that made the idea more palatable because they stopped talking about *conquering*... Theirs were political movements that were supposedly *Of the People* and, therefore, conquering wasn't necessary. Their rule expanded by *liberating* the people of other cultures and freeing them from oppression... via revolution (the left has always been good at *branding*).[14]

Those are much prettier words used to describe the same desire to rule the world. What revolutionaries such as Karl Marx camouflage when describing their Utopian paradise is the fact that there will still be a politburo or Ruling Class that actually run things.[15]

The modern day Globalists are even more subtle. They prefer to leave people with the appearance of sovereignty. If Globalism is discussed, it is always in economic terms – seldom in political terms (at least at first – look at the European Union as an example).[16]

But make no mistake, the political power inherent in Globalism has attracted that same element that thirsts for control over others. Globalism has an entire chapter of this book dedicated to it, but for now we need to realize that the race over who will control the world is well under way...

Understand this... Globalism is probably inevitable. As economic markets become more interdependent, as technology and advanced communications shrink the planet, global cooperation will lead to global regulation which will lead to *de facto* governance.[17]

The issue is not whether we'll eventually have a global government; the issue is, *What type of government will it be?*

As is explained in this book and on the StressFreeBill.com website, the self-appointed **Ruling Class** that has been running America for the last decade or so see the profit and opportunity in Globalism. They are blinded and corrupted by it.

And that brings us to the fourth simple truth:

Globalism and the Constitution of the United States of America are not compatible.

Or, more accurately, our Constitution is not compatible with the socialistic version of globalism the Ruling Class is currently attempting to cram down our throat.

For the Globalist's vision to come true, America must be subordinate to a higher governing authority. Ideas of individual liberty, inalienable rights, and protections against religious persecution (among many other things) cannot be allowed to survive intact.[18] Even our concept of property rights would need to be modified.

What is happening in America today is not a new story. The opponents of liberty are smarter and more subtle, but their objectives are still the same. They want to rule the world and *We the People* are standing in their way.

Just to be clear... StressFreeBill has no problem with a world government – as long as it's our government. A government *Of the People, By the People, and For the People.*

The globalism we're being forced into today bears no resemblance to that...

CHAPTER THREE

It's Not About Issues - It's About Freedom

Americans young and old, political or apolitical, liberal or conservative have long felt that we have lost control of our government, that our voice and our vote doesn't really matter.[1] Some would go as far as to proclaim that the game is rigged, while others (not wanting to sound extreme) claim that it's not quite that bad, yet scratch their heads when asked how to give more control back to the people...[2]

Here is the truth – the game *is* rigged.

We're not talking about crazy ideas of secretive groups like the Trilateral Commission controlling everything. The self-appointed **Ruling Class** that has been running America for decades doesn't hold secret meetings or have secret handshakes. They don't elect officers or vote on an agenda...

What we have is more of a *profession-based* **Ruling Class** akin to what the great philosopher Plato called for in his writing, The Republic.[3] Plato advocates for a society where the 'best and the brightest' are called on to lead and are then given the legal and moral authority to do so. His is an oligarchical society where the only rights the citizenry hold are those bestowed by their elitist leaders.

In modern times, we have seen many versions of this philosophy lead to disaster. Communism, Fascism, Nazism, Totalitarianism, and the most common version, Socialism (like what we see playing out in Venezuela), have led to more human tragedy than any other forms of government. It can even be argued that Monarchies (having a King and/or Queen) have been relatively kinder to their people than Plato's vision. Kings have certainly slain fewer people.

In America, however, certain groups of people have come to believe they represent our 'best and brightest.' These groups have slowly risen to power and sunk deep roots in their respective institutions. For years, they have run the country by exercising power in their respective professions and/or by manipulating voters to elect politicians that reflect their worldview.

They fully believe they know better how to run the country than you, and feel morally justified in subverting your voice. It is important to understand that this sense of professional superiority gives them full license to ignore the US Constitution and the traditions and history behind it. To them, the ends justify the means and they will wield power over you by any means necessary. *Lying to your face* is the least of the sins these people are willing to commit to ensure their superior rule over you.

In other words, this self-appointed Ruling Class has come to self-righteously believe Plato was right. The fact that over and over again throughout history Plato's vision for government has led to misery, slavery, and despair apparently escapes them in their heady hold on power (or, they just don't care).

To most Americans, this flies in the face of everything we believe in. We immediately find ourselves searching for other motivations because this way of thinking is so foreign to what we know. To most of us, the idea that only members of certain professions have the training, education, and informational access to make good policy decisions and law is anathema to our thinking; to think that only a certain class of people should be allowed to have a say on how our country is run is laughable. Yet, this is their groupthink.

How can so many people that have never met, from a number of different professions, separated by generation, geography, and even political affiliation hold such a common mass delusion? The answer to that question is the missing link that prevents most rational thinking people from seeing the (new) big picture. Without an understanding of this dynamic, our minds simply reject the reality as wild conspiracy... So, are you ready? The reason all those different people can work together so seamlessly *is because their sense of superiority has become a culture; a culture that wasn't originated, but has now been adopted, financed, backed and promoted by the Ruling Class Oligarchy.* (We'll further discuss the Ruling Class Oligarchy in another chapter)

Most members of America's new self-appointed Ruling Class have never studied Plato and probably could not even articulate the reasoning behind their self-acknowledged superiority... It's just the way things *are*... It is *their truth*.

They are all living inside a cultural bubble where the constant feedback they get is self-confirming. So, they arrogantly believe they are smarter and/or better informed than you or the average voter. They believe guiding the rest of us is their obligation to humanity...

Therefore, it is extremely important *We the People* understand this argument is not about whether the self-appointed Ruling Class has good ideas or not; this political revolution is being fought over *what kind* of government we will have. Will we have a government *Of the People, For the People, and By the People?*[4] Or, will we allow ourselves to be ruled by a relatively small group of elitists?

No government is perfect. *The Federalist style of Representative Democracy the US Constitution gives us is a terrible form of government – it is just far better than any other government in the history of mankind.* We have all watched *The People* collectively call for some stupid things before, but those instances pale in comparison to the atrocities committed by powerful Ruling Classes.

Some have described what is happening in America today as a *Soft Coup* – it is certainly an attempt to change our form of government.

It is my belief that most people on both sides of this conflict are not bad people - they are simply ignorant. That is not an insult; ignorance is simply a lack of knowledge - and the **Ruling Class Intelligentsia** is indoctrinating our children in *their* values while the **Ruling Class Media** is doing everything it can to keep them ignorant of ours.

The professions and organizations making up this Ruling Class are:

(This is a brief overview; each will be discussed in detail in subsequent chapters)

The Ruling Class Media - The mainstream media has lost all sense of fairness and now proclaims the right to tell us how to think (and vote).[5] [6] To accomplish this, they will literally publish and report Fake News they know to be false.[7] They are surrounded by editors and journalism professors that promote this type of *journalistic advocacy* and, therefore, literally don't know any better.[8] Their world is a feedback bubble where everyone around them thinks the same way - and anyone in flyover country that thinks differently must be unsophisticated and/or uneducated. They arrogantly believe *'the masses'* have *'no clue'* and it is their duty to manipulate us. They place their own chase for clicks and ratings ahead of the country and laugh at those that naively think this to be morally wrong. Do all media members deserve to be labeled as Ruling Class Media? No, but many do.

Ruling Class Politicians - They say whatever it takes to get elected, then proceed to ignore the will of their constituents. They don't work for *The People;* they work for the Ruling Class Oligarchs that have the money to keep them in office. Honesty is an elastic word to them. Fooling people has become a game to them. They have created all kinds of verbiage and legislative rules to give them cover.[9] Elections are not about Democrat vs Republican, *they are about Ruling Class Politicians vs outsiders.* This is why the Democratic National Committee (DNC) rigged the Primary against Bernie Sanders, and why you had a number of elected Republicans supporting Hillary Clinton over Donald Trump. To this day, many Republican Ruling Class politicians only pretend to support our President while actually seeking to undermine him at every turn. They are the definition of putting their own interests ahead of the country. Do all politicians deserve to be labeled as Ruling Class Politicians? No, but many do.

The Ruling Class Bureaucracy - This is the Deep State. Career and politically appointed bureaucrats that create and enforce regulations that fit their vision, regardless of the direction their elected bosses give them. Theirs is a professional arrogance based on their 'superior' experience and training. They are confident they know better than the average voter and our elected representatives what's good for the country. Their arrogance is so profound that they have recently gone as far as to commit felonies by leaking classified information to undermine a duly elected US President.[10] They do not care that these leaks not only hurt our President but literally hurt our country as well.[11] Do all bureaucrats deserve to be labeled as the Ruling Class Bureaucracy? No, but many do.

The Ruling Class Intelligentsia - This group is made up of the self-acknowledged *most intelligent* elements in our society. These people generally earn their living by theorizing, not actually doing. This group is characterized by a visceral hatred of the United States and everything it stands for (They would deny this; they would classify their disdain as a *realistic* view of history, unsullied by concepts of patriotism). They work for Think Tanks, appear as consultants on TV, and populate the ranks of academia as professors, teachers and school administrators. Many of our Ruling Class Media, Ruling Class Politicians, and Ruling Class Judiciary have been educated, indoctrinated, and inspired by them. Does everyone in these groups deserve to be labeled as Ruling Class Intelligentsia? No, but many do.

The Ruling Class Judiciary - These are judges that have been indoctrinated to believe that the US Constitution can mean anything they want it to.[12] They literally believe that, as judges, they have the right to change its meaning to reflect their own 'smarter vision' for our society.[13] No longer constraining themselves to rule on the constitutionality of a written law, they have now declared themselves to be the arbiter of what elected leaders *are thinking*; they are now ruling based on what they speculate a leader's overall policy *motivation* to be.[14] Are all judges of the Ruling Class Judiciary? No, but many are.

The Ruling Class Oligarchy - This group is made up of CEOs, old-money philanthropists, wunderkind entrepreneurs, K Street lobbyists, Union bosses, and Political Action Committee (PAC) organizers. They use their wealth and influence to manipulate the political system (Think of people like George Soros and Mark Zuckerberg).[15] [16] Do all of these individuals deserve to be labeled as Ruling Class Oligarchs? No, but many do.

Ruling Class Suck-ups - These are people that have gained fame and celebrity and attempt to use it publicly in support of the Ruling Class. Their understanding of the issues tends to be shallow, but they are desperate to be seen as proud members of 'the right crowd' – think of the 'popular' kids in high school. In general, this group is so manipulated they have no idea they are supporting the Ruling Class agenda. Hollywood and professional sports provide most of this group. Do all celebrities deserve to be labeled as Ruling Class Suck-ups? No, but a whole lot of them do.

CHAPTER FOUR

Understanding that Government Is Not Our Friend

Our Founding Fathers knew better...

Before we go any further in our narrative, it is important to address this issue. We have had a number of generations now (including the Millennials) raised in the doctrine that the purpose of government is to take care of us. They have been taught to look at government as a father-like paternal figure that is there to *pick us up and dust us off* when we fall down and to protect us against anything *really* bad happening against us. This is the mindset behind the drive for single-payer healthcare, the ever-continuing expansion of Medicaid, Gun Control, ever-increasing government regulations, Public Housing, expanding the food stamp program, the Environmental Protection Agency (EPA) expansion, etc. Reduced to basic simplicity, the mindset reads; *Government is here to prevent anything bad from happening to us.* The corollary to that is; *The bigger and more powerful the government is, the less bad that can happen.*

But who really believes this?

Perhaps it would be more accurate to say that this is the *justification* the Ruling Class pushes to buy the votes of those indoctrinated to naively believe these are valid functions of government.

In fact, the only valid functions of government are to provide services for the common good that are totally impractical or impossible to achieve in any other way.

To believe differently is to ignore the vast sum of human experience that proves otherwise... Historically, government has *always* been a greater force for evil than good.

This doesn't mean that everyone shouldn't have access to healthcare, or that there shouldn't be a safety net in place for emergency situations, but unless we are talking about a last-ditch backstop, the private sector has always been much better at providing these things. In the United States, government long ago passed the point where it was providing needed welfare services; its current expansion simply takes over services being previously provided by charities, churches, and other private organizations. In other words, government welfare is now expanding simply for the sake of expansion; it is not fulfilling any great unmet needs of the citizenry.

And this is a grievous mistake. Any honorable historian will tell you it is a mistake to feed the beast.

Our country was founded by people fleeing the oppressive governments of Europe (Yes, the Indians were already here, but they didn't trust big governments either – point made).

Europeans had good reason not to trust government. Up until that time, Kings, Queens, and a few Emperors had mostly run everything. And it had worked out well... if you were the King, Queen, or Emperor (or, of the Ruling Class they established around them). For centuries, there was little chance for the common man to rise through the ranks and improve his or her station in life. StressFreeBill is sure that parents still told their children, "You can grow up to be anything you want – as long as you want to be a farmer" (or whatever trade your father practiced).

You can actually look throughout Asia, South America, Africa, and the rest of the world and find the same thing. But whether spelled out in some complex code of law or if it was just a tribal Chieftain threatening to kill you if you didn't do what you were told; all governments have had one thing in common – absolute control over the masses.

And then, somewhere around the 1770s in the colonies of the New World, a crazy idea started taking hold. An idea that said it's always been backwards – that it should be *the people* that have absolute control over their government, not the other way around. Thus, the crown jewel of Western Civilization was born.

StressFreeBill isn't going to chronicle the entire American Revolution here, but it should not be forgotten that massive amounts of progress have occurred since that concept for government took hold. Technology, Standards of Living, healthcare, reduction of poverty, elimination of illiteracy, increased lifespans – the quality of life itself has gone up for billions of people (both inside and outside of our country) *because* that concept of government was put into practice.

All of this unparalleled explosion of activity and innovation occurred because government, for the first time in history, was constrained and severely limited in its authority over the masses. And the only authority that could decide how much control the government could have was *The People* themselves.

And for the first time in history, the entire world benefited – not just the small group in power.

They called the United States Government an experiment, because it had never been done before.[1] And like all good experiments it proved something; it proved that government is the force that holds humanity back from greater things. It proved that government must be constrained. It proved that government controlled by the many was far superior to government controlled by the few.

Of course, there are always those who want to challenge that.

In the two hundred plus years since the United States was founded, many self-appointed intellectual elites (or, power hungry despots – depending on your point of view) have declared that *they* could do it better. They agree that government must be for *The People*, but if given the authority they can better manage it for us (I kid you not!). That they and their small group of elitists could run government far better, far more efficiently, and much more *fairly* (they always throw that in to make it sound better). These intellectual giants have founded governments based on Communism, Fascism, Nazism, and Socialism (among others).

Not only have they never come close to equaling the progress the United States gave humanity, the world has never seen such misery and carnage as what these managers have wrought.

There is a two-word truism or adage that sums this up perfectly…

Power corrupts.

The Founding Fathers, StressFreeBill, and everyone with half a brain realizes that some government is necessary. But it is like the man-eating tiger at the zoo – you take no chances on letting it escape. Government should remain as restricted as possible – it should never be given more authority than what it absolutely needs to maintain society.

It is totally understandable for good men and women to disagree and debate where those limits on government should be, but when StressFreeBill starts hearing Ruling Class Politicians and the Ruling Class Intelligentsia teaching our children that government is their friend… this represents a danger to us all.[2][3]

All government is evil – it is just a necessary evil.

The Founding Fathers understood this. *The United States Constitution* and, especially, *The Bill of Rights* do not discuss the rights of government... they discuss the rights of citizens to be protected *from* government.[4] [5]

StressFreeBill can sum it up this way...

The Representative Democracy used in the United States is the worst form of government on Earth – except for all the others.

No government is perfect (or even close) but, as long as we restrain and control it, we have the best form in existence. But make no mistake – our government is not our friend. If we become lazy in keeping the cage locked, if we become lulled by the whispers of those that would use its authority to 'manage' us... *We the People* will be devoured.

In the following chapters, we will take a look at the various groups that don't know or don't care about what we just discussed...

CHAPTER FIVE

The Ruling Class Media

"If you know the enemy and know yourself, you need not fear the result of a hundred battles. If you know yourself but not the enemy, for every victory gained you will also suffer a defeat. If you know neither the enemy nor yourself, you will succumb in every battle."
- Sun Tzu, The Art of War

Many people refer to them as the mainstream media; others call them the leftist media or the national media...

We should all start calling them the Ruling Class Media.

> **Ruling Class Media** noun / ruː.lɪŋ ˈklæs ˈmid·i·ə/
> Media personnel that arrogantly believe 'the masses' have 'no clue' and it is for our own good that they manipulate us. Their arrogant

assumption of intellectual superiority gives them license to eschew traditional journalistic standards. They place their own chase for clicks and ratings ahead of the country and laugh at those that naively think this to be morally wrong.

Branding is how we fight back.

Does every journalist fit this definition? No, of course not. But if everyone would start referring to the ones that do as the **Ruling Class Media**, it would immediately disempower their influence over many. *Ruling Class* conveys arrogance and the desire to control and manipulate - all things that Americans rightfully resent. It would stick because it has become a *truism* - something that is immediately recognized as truth. StressFreeBill would love to watch George Stephanopoulos or Chuck Todd struggle to explain how they are not part of the Ruling Class Media.

Words are important. Wars are won with bullets; culture is won with language.

Branding them is easy; understanding them is harder.

There are (at least) two dynamics at play when it comes to understanding today's Ruling Class Media. First, most are young and have been indoctrinated by the **Ruling Class Intelligentsia**. Many in this generation of journalists aren't bad people, they just literally don't know any better.

Like attracts like and for decades now we have allowed our best universities to be bastions of the left. No longer institutions where all ideologies are represented, they are churning out generation after generation of graduates that do not believe in Capitalism, competition, or self-reliance and personal responsibility. With a skewed understanding of history, many are taught that America is no better than any other country and we have no right to exert our will on others (to lead). They're taught that to believe in the goodness of America is morally hypocritical. Concepts of good and evil become relative under this worldview and to hold out America's history of freedom and achievement as a force for good is considered laughably naive.

If the faculty of Ivy League Universities is heavily populated by the left, their colleges of journalism are even more so. Both before and after graduation these individuals are immersed in the groupthink. It would take an extraordinarily strong-willed individual (and probably a very discreet one) to maintain an independent and open mind against this hourly barrage of single-sided ideology.

This leads to the second dynamic: Censorship and Sensationalism.

Their claims to be unbiased are disingenuous.[1] News stories that don't fit their narrative simply go unreported.[2]

When it comes to hyping news that does fit their narrative, StressFreeBill believes most journalists simply kill two birds with one stone by sensationalizing. They get the professional benefit of better ratings and the personal satisfaction of guiding (manipulating) the public to their *greater truth...*

While many in the Ruling Class Media look at *We the People* as unfairly patriotic and hopelessly naive, they are also enthralled with their own race for personal success.

Sensationalism sells newspapers, so to speak.

And when you've been taught that morality is not absolute but relative, why wouldn't ethics be also?

Those that quickly rise to the national ranks in journalism (like Ivy Leaguers) are also exposed to the rich and powerful **Ruling Class Oligarchs** - some of whom own the very institutions they work for.[3] These movers and shakers sing an irresistible siren's song and find an easily moldable audience among the Ruling Class Media. Some speak of being all-inclusive and having a world without borders (while harboring the hidden agenda of desiring a huge influx of new voters for the Democrat party). Others talk about Compassionate Conservatism (while reaping increased profits from the lower wages illegal immigration brings).

Just accept what they tell you at face value and sing the 'company line' to watch your personal fortunes soar, or (else)...

If there was ever a group of people to feel sorry for, it would be America's current cadre of Ruling Class Media.

There are certainly journalists among them that hate America and everything it stands for, and they would love to see us knocked down to everyone else's level in a global system. But StressFreeBill suspects that most are simply victims - they are the truly naive of our society. They are naive because they have never really been credibly exposed to diverse ways of thinking and have been humored and manipulated since they were mere children leaving high school.

Whether a person is being manipulated or is the manipulator, however, it makes no difference. We must stand up to those that would destroy the laws, morals, ethics, and values that made our country great. We must unmask those that would undermine our way of government and way of life. We must name them for what they are: the **Ruling Class Media.**

The incredible power of creating this social meme will be discussed in a subsequent chapter.

CHAPTER SIX

The Ruling Class Intelligentsia

Of all the groups making up America's self-appointed Ruling Class, the Ruling Class Intelligentsia is the group StressFreeBill has the most disdain for.

He has been known to refer to them as educated idiots, dupes, and... other things.

Throughout history, the Ruling Class Oligarchy has supported the Intelligentsia Class.[1] Merlin of King Author's Court could be considered of the Intelligentsia. Later in Europe, during the Renaissance Period, Kings and Queens often included in their court astrologers, mathematicians, alchemists, painters, advisors, and philosophers – as much for amusement as practical value to the kingdom.

One distinguishing characteristic of this group is that it was very difficult to survive without the support of a patron. In other words, the free market didn't value their contributions enough to afford most of them a living. Without the financial support of a king (government), most of this class wouldn't have existed.

This still holds true today – Without financial donations to Think Tanks, Universities, etc., most of our Ruling Class Intelligentsia would disappear. Most of their salaries derive from the patronage of the Ruling Class Oligarchy, or from the taxpayer.

It is very important to note that StressFreeBill is not disdainful of all intelligentsia, only our *Ruling Class Intelligentsia*. Galileo was part of the Intelligentsia as are some of our brightest thinkers today. However, in America, the *Ruling Class* Intelligentsia has become dominate…

> **Ruling Class Intelligentsia** noun / ru:.lɪŋ 'klæs 'in-tel-i-jent-see-uh/
> This is a large group of educated persons engaged in the complex mental labors that critique, guide, and lead in shaping the culture and politics of our society. What separates them from other intellectuals is their absolute belief in their own superiority. They believe they fit the definition of Plato's 'best and brightest' and therefore arrogantly ignore *We the People* as intellectually unfit to make decisions. As a class, the intelligentsia includes professors, teachers, and other academics, pundits, Think Tanks, community organizers, and the literary Hommes de Lettres.

The Ruling Class Intelligentsia is responsible for indoctrinating our current wave of Ruling Class Media. They have educated and trained the Ruling Class Bureaucracy that infests the higher levels of our Federal Agencies. They have filled student's minds with anti-American and anti-Capitalism beliefs. They extoll the virtues of Socialism while hypocritically ignoring the real disasters it results in (like Venezuela and Greece). They have given intellectual cover to our Ruling Class Politicians and promoted the idea of moral relativism that has warped the thinking of our Ruling Class Judiciary.[2]

On a cultural level, the Ruling Class Intelligentsia has now taught generations of students that it is okay to take to the streets and that violence can be a means to an end... That 'Hate Speech' should not be considered Free Speech and hate is whatever the 'Politically Correct' say it is. They have led the crusade against Christianity and demanded that government shun it (which was never the intent of the Founding Fathers). They have promoted victimization and identity politics, using race, gender, sexual preference, and religion to divide us as a nation.[3] They focus on the inevitable imperfections of America rather than on our unparalleled record of offering freedom, raising standards of living, empowering personal achievement, and opposing dictatorial forces worldwide.

In short, the Ruling Class Intelligentsia has done everything it can to destroy the traditions and values of America.

They have also shown themselves to be incompetent...

It is ironic that these arrogant self-appointed arbiters of what's best for all of us have never actually done anything themselves...

The Ruling Class Intelligentsia are (mostly) people that sit back and tell you how to do things they've never done before. You know the type... we used to call them *'Know-it-alls.'*

How can you dictate to politicians with certainty how to create millions of jobs if you've never even created *one* yourself? If you've never hired anyone before, how can you possibly understand the difficulties and challenges involved?

How can you negotiate multi-billion dollar trade deals if you've never before even had to negotiate a lease for an office?

And these are the people training everyone else how to run our country!

Regardless of which side of the Republican vs Democrat game you spend most of your time on, even the most partisan among us would have to recognize the terrible performance of the Obama economy.[4] Obama supporters even recognized it and preached to us that it was the best we could expect – that averaging less than 2% annual GDP growth was the *new normal.*[5]

Just a quick look at President Obama's cabinet can give us insight – it was stuffed with Ruling Class Intelligentsia.[6] Remember the old adage... *Those who can't, teach...*

When talking about Public School teachers StressFreeBill always has to walk a fine line...

As a society, we need our teachers and should honor them.

StressFreeBill has a sister that teaches kindergarten and is a finalist for Teacher of the Year in her home state. Is she a member of the Ruling Class Intelligentsia? No. And it is doubtful that many kindergarten teachers are. But when StressFreeBill, during the 2012 election, can walk into a public high school classroom in Plano, TX and witness Obama campaign posters, and the teacher passing out Obama campaign buttons... That history teacher - and the administration that permitted his behavior - is part of the Ruling Class Intelligentsia. Good teachers teach students how to think – not arrogantly dictate what their political conclusions should be. True intellectuals offer ideas and accept debate – the Ruling Class Intelligentsia arrogantly insists they are smarter than you and there is no need for debate – and they will use their positions of authority to pressure or intimidate you into compliance.

Whether it is a liberal college professor at the local Junior College or one of the so-called conservative editors at the National Review, the cultural feedback bubble they live in leaves them oblivious to the embarrassing arrogance they publically display.

If they weren't doing so much damage to the country you could almost feel sorry for the Ruling Class Intelligentsia...

Pick any network or cable channel – FOX, CNN, MSNBC, etc. – and listen to the Ruling Class Intelligentsia pundits being interviewed about the issues of the day. They always get it wrong. They are always wrong because they always frame their arguments in terms of Republican vs Democrat, or conservative vs progressive. That's not what it's about.

They are the pawns of the Ruling Class Oligarchs and most of them don't even realize it; many of them probably believe they are supported because of their keen intellect. In reality, the Ruling Class Oligarchy support them because the derision they sow helps break down American Sovereignty and brings them closer to their globalist goals. So, make no mistake, they are merely puppets dancing to their puppet masters' strings. The majority of Ruling Class Oligarchs couldn't care less about the environment, or racial justice, or compassionate conservatism, or even the Constitution of the United States. But they are more than happy to let their puppets dance away and advocate whatever they want – as long as it also supports the globalist agenda.

StressFreeBill wants Americans to stop being pulled into this charade. It is time we name the real enemy and call them out for what they really are – *Ruling Class Intelligentsia* and *Ruling Class Oligarchs*… aka anti-American globalists.

CHAPTER SEVEN

Ruling Class Politicians

StressFreeBill is not a person that believes all politicians are evil people. Many are hard-working family men and women that began their careers in public service with a desire to serve the greater good. Along the way, however, many get subverted, or *indoctrinated*, into the Ruling Class culture. This cultural assimilation is most prevalent on a national level but not restricted to it.

Simply put, they lose touch with the basic values of the people that originally voted them into office. Somewhere along the way *believing in things* became less important than *knowing the right people*. The more cynical among us might say that a politician would never have been successful if his or her heart hadn't always been dark, but I prefer to believe this is not true – at least not for everyone. I also prefer to believe that not everyone is corrupted by holding national public office, but evidence and observation show that sadly many are.

The problem is the very fact that holding political office has become a *profession*. Public Service was supposed to be just that – a service. Being elected a representative of the people was an honor and a duty... Not career advancement.[1]

I prefer to deal with reality, however, so let's talk about the way things *are*...

> **Ruling Class Politicians** noun / ru:.lɪŋ 'klæs 'pälə'tiSHəns//
> A professional ruling class that feigns allegiance to a constituency while pursuing other agendas. Using their legislative power, they have gamed the system to enhance their personal riches and protect themselves from public scrutiny. They carry a cultural arrogance that, in their minds, places them above the people they rule.

Ruling Class Politicians are those with a higher priority than serving their constituents.

Their priority is to serve the people that can get them reelected. And more often than not, those people are the Ruling Class Oligarchy, the Ruling Class Media, and the Ruling Class Intelligentsia.

It is a sad fact of life in the United States that almost half of all eligible citizens don't exercise their right to vote.[2] And of those that do, most don't pay close attention to the issues. They are referred to by various names: low information voters, the masses, denizens of flyover country, etc. Our Founding Fathers called them, *We the People*. Most in this demographic 'stick their heads up' around election time, get a feel for what's going on, vote, and then go back to what is understandably more important in their lives.

These people are looked at by the Ruling Class Media as easy to manipulate.

Over recent years the Ruling Class Media has demonstrated this ability with ever-increasing success. Think about how they were able to protect President Bill Clinton from acts of perjury and President Barack Obama from scandals at the VA, IRS, ATF, and State Department. This ability to make or break politicians has given them a heady power that has attracted the attention of the Ruling Class Oligarchs. Indeed, as mentioned elsewhere in this book, the largest national media in this country are owned by only about six companies and controlled by only a handful of families.[3] In later chapters we will discuss some contributing factors as to how this came about, but for the purposes of understanding Ruling Class Politicians we must accept that, for the most part, the hold the media has over them is very real. Our politicians certainly believe it to be true.

For my entire lifetime the media has been biased. But what we're seeing today goes well beyond simple ideology.[4] There is now an elitist arrogance in the media that has allowed it to drop all pretense of fairness. They no longer simply report the news; they *shape* the news.

While they publicly claim to be unbiased, they don't really believe it or care. And while they are on the public record as overwhelmingly one sided in their political donations (Democrat), party affiliation is not something they see as particularly important...

They believe they are *above* politics.

Theirs is a greater truth. They are citizens of the world, and ideas of patriotism and nationalism are at best quaint, but more likely silly and naïve. To the Ruling Class Media, politicians of either party are either insiders that share their lofty views, or outsiders that deserve only pro forma respect (and many times not even that).

Again, we're not talking about a conspiracy... We're talking about a culture. A culture that is very seductive to politicians that are looking to build a career and provide a better life for themselves and their families. It also doesn't hurt that they are bubbled into that culture – their workplace, the parties they attend, even the restaurants they frequent are inundated with persons that share that same elitist cultural view.[5] In a perfect world we would only elect representatives with high moral standards, good character, and the strongest strength of will (all of which are necessary to stand up to what they are subjected to). Unfortunately, we don't tend to be that discerning when casting our votes. Therefore a huge number, possibly the majority, of our national politicians are Ruling Class Politicians.

It is so important to understand the incestuous relationship between the Ruling Class Media and our Ruling Class Politicians that StressFreeBill will dedicate the next chapter to giving an actual example of how Ruling Class Politicians give themselves cover from the electorate, and how the Ruling Class Media allows the charade to go unchallenged.

How, you might ask, does StressFreeBill know these things to be true?

It's a fair question, and here's a fair answer... These are the things *I* believe to be true based upon close observation, an extensive and experienced understanding of human nature, and ongoing analysis of behavior. Remember, *Behavior Never Lies.* Some readers will immediately recognize these words as truth. Either because they've already come to the same conclusions themselves, or because they experience an *Ah Ha!* moment (when suddenly it all makes sense).

I encourage everyone to start closely watching politicians and members of the media with my explanations for behavior in mind. My guess is it won't take more than a week to start seeing through all the pretenses and subterfuge.

Ruling class politicians must be exposed and opposed... And ultimately voted out of office.

This is where *We the People* need to be strong. It makes little difference whether your favorite politician is a crook or simply a victim of the system, if their behavior shows them to be a Ruling Class Politician they are leading us to disaster and we can no longer follow them. If the Ruling Class agenda continues unabated more and more of our freedoms will disappear. Surveillance of our private lives will increase, our rights to free speech will decrease, and our abilities to protect ourselves physically and economically will be taken away. The Ruling Class will become ever more firmly entrenched and history shows us where that will lead.

Our very freedom is at stake.

As I write this, reports of attempted political assassination fill the news. A crazed lunatic shot a number of people as senators and congressmen were practicing for a charity baseball game. StressFreeBill does not condone this, or any violence, to oppose the Ruling Class. Two points, however, need to be made...

First, we must realize that revolutions historically occur when the populace feels they no longer have a voice. Frustration grows as control over one's destiny is taken away. Whether real or imagined, when the people feel unrepresented they lash out.

Secondly, all good people that love and care about the future of our country must avoid this frustration. The Rule of Law is what has allowed this country to be great; it's what has allowed us to have our freedoms and lead ourselves and the world to greater prosperity. If we are to save our country we must preserve the Rule of Law. We cannot act outside it. We can and will overcome the insidious attempts of the Ruling Class by working within the framework of our political system. In the end, *We the People* will have proven to be the faction of superior discipline, intellect and character.

CHAPTER EIGHT

How Congress Gets Away With Lying To Us

Not all Senators and Congressmen are crooks, but many might as well be... If you consider taking taxpayer dollars for salary and expenses under false pretenses to be crooked, then many are very, very guilty.

Ruling Class Politicians do not want to make the changes we elected them to make and the Ruling Class Media gives them cover because they don't want the status quo altered either. But they have to give themselves some kind of excuse... so how do they do it?

One great example is called the Byrd Rule.[1]

Named after former West Virginia Senator Robert Byrd, this is a Senate Rule that basically states the minority party can prevent most types of legislation from passing unless the majority can muster 60 votes (60% majority). This almost never happens.

So, GOP Senators can wring their hands and lament that even though they currently hold a 52-48 majority, they just can't get those important things they promised passed.[2] Darn it!

In addition, it gives our GOP leaders in the House of Representatives great cover to renege on promises as well – even though they hold an even bigger majority in Congress. They simply lament, "Gee, we can't pass that bill because it would never get through the Senate!" So, they don't even vote – and the reneging politicians never have to actually go on record as opposing their promises.

A great bonus for these same GOP leaders is that it lets them act heroic in trying to frame a bill that will qualify to avoid the 60-vote Byrd Rule threshold – via something called Reconciliation.[3] "Boy, we worked so hard to try and figure out how to do this… it's too bad that in the end we just couldn't pull it off."

The **Ruling Class Media** then legitimizes these excuses by interviewing pundits, consultants, and others from the **Ruling Class Intelligentsia** as they explain ad nauseam how difficult it would be to get 60 votes for that particular bill.

Here's the nasty little secret…

The GOP could get rid of the Byrd Rule faster than you can snap your fingers…*if they wanted to.*

You see, *it's just a rule*. It's not a law. It's not mentioned in the US Constitution. It's not even a centuries-old tradition. The Senate Rules have changed often over its 200+ year history. Senate Leader Mitch

McConnell could call for a simple majority vote and it would be gone![2]

So, why doesn't he do it? *My strong intuition tells me he doesn't want to.* It gives all of the **Ruling Class Politicians** (on both sides of the aisle) cover for all of the above-mentioned reasons.

Are we sure he could do this? Yes. Because they already did...

The Democrats did it in 2013, and remember the Supreme Court nomination of Neil Gorsuch?[4] The Democrats promised they would never allow the GOP to get 60 votes – so McConnell changed the rules (for Supreme Court nominations only).[5] I think even our **Ruling Class Politicians** realized the American People wouldn't buy their excuses if they blew that one...

But, the point is, all he has to do is change the rule.[2]

So, how does he *justify* not changing the rule?

Senator McConnell and other Ruling Class Politicians will tell you that this rule is a safeguard against the majority having too much power and that he doesn't want to set the precedent of changing it because, when the Democrats gain the majority, he doesn't want the GOP to be powerless.[2]

The first part – *the majority having too much power*– is absurd. Elections have consequences and this is just a weak excuse for not enacting the will of the people.

The second part – wanting to maintain the standard for when the majority changes – sounds really good... until you realize that it is a false premise. *The precedent has already been set and the first thing the Democrats will do when they gain the majority is to remove the Byrd Rule!* We know this because former Senate Majority Leader Harry Reid (D-NV) told us so.[6]

Even without Reid tipping everyone off as to their plans, does anyone really believe the Democrats would show any restraint in their exercise of power? Even Las Vegas wouldn't take a bet on that – at any odds.

I defy any politician or media personality to give StressFreeBill a rational explanation for the GOP to preserve this rule. I will give them space on my website at www.StressFreeBill.com and post their response for all to see. But, I'm not going to hold my breath...

So, the next time you hear Speaker of the House Paul Ryan talk about why repealing Obamacare is so complicated, or how tax reform is going to take a lot of time and compromise, remember... it's all a smokescreen to cover America's self-appointed **Ruling Class** from enacting the Will of the People.[7]

They know they are superior to you and, therefore, only owe you lip service (to get your vote). If that makes you mad...

Well, yeah... it should.

CHAPTER NINE

Ruling Class Oligarchs

These are powerful people in America. Their power derives from vast wealth, or more specifically, the control of vast wealth. Some hail from 'old money families' while others represent Wunderkind entrepreneurs like the founder of Facebook, Mark Zuckerburg.[1] Many are CEOs of multinational corporations or managers of hedge funds, Reserve Banks, and Investment Banks. The junior leagues of this group include the still very powerful K Street lobbyists, some Union Bosses, and Political Action Committee (PAC) organizers.[2]

> **Ruling Class Oligarchy** noun / ruː.lɪŋ ˈklæs ˈol-i-gahr-kee /
> A relatively small group of very powerful people that place their own interests ahead of any country, ideology, or set of morals and standards. They successfully use their massive wealth and influence to manipulate the political system to achieve their ends.

It is very important to note that not all highly successful, highly wealthy, or extremely powerful people should be thought of as Ruling Class Oligarchs. To interpret this book as advocating class warfare would be missing the point. It is StressFreeBill's opinion that most people in this category are hard-working, good, and generous people. But there are definitely a number of them that seek power for a vision that has nothing to do with *We the People.*

Most Americans have no idea how powerful this group is...

To put the power of this small group into perspective, realize that 90% of the media in the United States is owned *by just six corporations...* and these corporations are controlled by only a handful of families.[3] [4]

Expanding internationally is the Holy Grail for most Ruling Class Oligarchs – that is where all the new profits are.

They benefit tremendously when tariffs and trade barriers are removed. Their profits increase when given unencumbered access to virgin markets and allowed to use cheap foreign labor without regard to humanitarian or environmental concerns. In other words, their wealth and power increase dramatically when allowed to exploit the Third World.

What's more, Nation States become an inconvenience when operating on this scale. Every country with its own set of regulations, currency, etc.

disrupts profits. It would be much easier for multi-national interests if individual countries would dissolve their sovereignty and merge into a common system (like the European countries did with the European Union).

Ruling Class Oligarchs are pure Globalists.

For many in the Ruling Class Oligarchy, political ideology is unimportant and is used as a tool to manipulate others. They couldn't care less which political party is 'in power.'

The Democrat Party supports the reduction of US sovereignty via open borders, amnesty, and illegal immigration as well as through accords such as the Paris Climate Treaty.

The Libertarian Party supports the reduction of US sovereignty via open borders, amnesty, and illegal immigration.

Many establishment Republican politicians are on record to, in effect, reduce US sovereignty by supporting open borders, amnesty, and illegal immigration as well as by supporting accords such as the Paris Climate Treaty.

Is it just a coincidence all parties mirror the agenda of the globalist Ruling Class Oligarchy?

Charles and David Koch are multi-billionaire Libertarians that have historically donated heavily to Republican candidates that support Immigration Reform (i.e. amnesty, open borders, etc.). For the first time in recent memory, they refused to support the

Republican nominee for President (who coincidently didn't support an open border agenda).[5]

George Soros is a multi-billionaire that funds a huge number of Democrat organizations that are almost exclusively trying to tear down American Sovereignty.[6] Several of these organizations have been reported to support and fund violent protests against *America First* conservatives and *controlled border* politicians.[7]

They both, along with many others in the Ruling Class Oligarchy, directly and indirectly, fund political candidates that support their globalist agenda. They may or may not believe in the rest of the silly stuff their parties advocate. StressFreeBill suspects that many of them are indifferent.

The Ruling Class Oligarchy doesn't care what type of government America (or the world) has – they play at a level above governments.

So, the next time we see a protester calling everyone a fascist, or a politician citing compassion as a reason not to enforce immigration law, or a former Republican Presidential Candidate like Mitt Romney professing concern for the environment as the US pulls out of the Paris Climate Treaty... remember, there is a good chance that the people pulling their strings couldn't care less about any of it.

In the eyes of the Ruling Class Oligarchy, politicians, pundits, illegal immigrants, and *We the People* are all just tools to be manipulated.

Are you starting to get fed-up? Hang on... it gets worse...

CHAPTER TEN

Who Is George Soros?

If you've ever watched a Batman, Wonder Woman, or Superman movie, then you know our superheroes are always pitted against a Super Villain - an individual or organization that is intent on ruling the world. Immensely wealthy and powerful, these individuals and their organizations are always motivated by greed and a lust for power. Although they may camouflage themselves as philanthropists or do-gooders, love for their fellow man is never part of the villains' make up. Come to think of it, you could include all the foes of James Bond as well as Ethan Hunt and his Mission Impossible team into that evil group, as well.

Why is it that so many children are attracted to these movies? Why is it so many children imagine themselves being Superman or Wonder Woman? I would suggest that a big part of it has to do with the fact that these stories tend to frame the fight of *Good versus Evil* in black and white terms. Superman represents everything good; the villain represents everything bad...

And what is everything bad portrayed as? Someone that wants to take over the world...

The super villains are always orchestrating and financing disruption, violence, and mayhem. They have elaborate schemes to achieve their ends and don't let things like the law, morals, or ethics stand in their way. Indeed, to them the ends justify the means and violence and the loss of life seem the least of their concerns.

StressFreeBill does not claim to be able to read the minds or know the hearts of any individual – he has enough trouble, at times, in understanding his own. But the philosophy, *Behavior Never Lies*, is a useful tool when it comes to understanding geopolitics. For our purposes, intent doesn't matter... Only behavior and the predictable results of that behavior. And there are public figures in our world whose *behavior* places them squarely in the camp of the Evil Villains. We call them Ruling Class Oligarchs.

According to Wikipedia:

> **George Soros** (/ˈsɔːroʊs/ or /ˈsɔːrɒs/; Hungarian: Soros György, pronounced [ˈʃoroʃ ˈɟørɟ]; born August 12, 1930) is a Hungarian-American investor, business magnate, philanthropist, and author. Soros is considered by some to be one of the most successful investors in the world. As of May 2017, Soros has a net worth of $25.2 billion making him one of the 30 richest people in the world.

Based on the facts, you can decide for yourself if George Soros is the epitome of a Ruling Class Oligarch. Not because he's rich, but because of what he does with his riches...

Although he was naturalized as a US citizen in 1961, he is on record as having anti-American and anti-capitalism views. For example in his book, <u>The Age of Fallibility</u>, he states, "the main obstacle to a stable and just world order is the United States.[1]" He goes on to discuss how the US 'war on terror' is misguided (you can't make this stuff up). He also blames free-market fundamentalism for many of the world's problems including the inhibition of economic development in Third World countries.

The website DiscoverTheNetworks.org introduces him thusly:

> New York hedge fund manager George Soros is one of the most politically powerful individuals on earth. Since the mid-1980s in particular, he has used his immense influence to help reconfigure the political landscapes of several countries around the world—in some cases playing a key role in toppling regimes that had held the reins of government for years, even decades. Vis à vis the United States, a strong case can be made for the claim that Soros today affects American politics and culture more profoundly that any other living person.

Much of Soros's influence derives from his $13 billion personal fortune, which is further leveraged by at least another $25 billion in investor assets controlled by his firm, Soros Fund Management. An equally significant source of Soros's power, however, is his passionate messianic zeal. Soros views himself as a missionary with something of a divine mandate to transform the world and its institutions into something better—*as he sees it.* (Emphasis added)

One of the ways in which he wants to transform the world is to curtail American sovereignty.[2] In his 1988 book, The Crisis of Global Capitalism: Open Society Endangered, he writes: *"Insofar as there are collective interests that transcend state boundaries, the sovereignty of states must be subordinated to international law and international institutions.[3]"* George Soros would like nothing more than for the United States to be subservient to international bodies such as the World Bank and the international monetary fund (IMF). He also supports and funds extreme environmentalists groups that advocate global jurisdiction. In his view, the United States is the evil Empire standing in the way of him reshaping the world in his image. Anything that would reduce the power, prestige, sovereignty, and influence of the United States of America is something worth funding and pursuing.

It is also worth noting that George Soros made much of his fortune during the Black Wednesday financial crisis in the United Kingdom. Known as *The*

Man Who Broke the Bank of England, he is credited/blamed for initiating that financial crisis.[4] He has been accused of currency manipulation and being an 'economic war criminal' in other parts of the world.[2] He is also a convicted felon in France.[4]

The list of radical political groups and activities that George Soros and his organizations fund both directly and indirectly would be extensive. But, to name a few:[5]

Black Lives Matter[6]
Occupy Wall Street[7]
Ferguson, MO Protests[8]
Standing Rock Protests[9]
Trump Campaign Rally Protests[10]
#NotMyPresident Protests[11]
The Women's March on Washington[12]
The Hillary Clinton Campaign[13] [14]
National Council of La Raza[15]
American Immigration Council
American Immigration Law Foundation
Arab American Institute Foundation
Aspen Institute
Black Alliance for Just Immigration
Brookings Institution
Democrat Party
Earthjustice
Grantmakers Without Borders
ACORN
Southern Poverty Law Center
Refuse Fascism[16]
Open Society[2]

Again, these are but a few of the radical groups George Soros, in one way or another, funds, contributes to, and supports. StressFreeBill would encourage everyone to take a few moments to Google these events and organizations. You may very well be shocked to discover that they represent *blatant* anti-Americanism, civil unrest, and disdain for the principals, ethics, and morals that the United States was founded upon.

Just what you would expect from the egotistical evil villain in a James Bond movie.

It is also what you would expect from an avowed globalist.

Remember, the Ruling Class Oligarchy will honor no law or tradition that would stand in the way of them subverting the *Will of the People*. George Soros personnel have been linked to attempting to undermine the election of President Donald Trump by scheming to manipulate the Electoral College.[17] They have 'helped' Facebook censor newsfeeds.[18] They filed lawsuits to halt President Trump's efforts to keep us safe by imposing a 90 day halt to immigration from dangerous countries.[19] [20] He has joined forces with President Barack Obama to resist and undermine President Donald Trump's agenda.[21]

Lest we get tempted to assume that George Soros is just a crazy socialist that supports the Democrat party, realize this... His organizations also funded Ruling Class Politicians on the Republican side of the aisle like Paul Ryan, Marco Rubio, Jeb Bush, John McCain,

John Kasich, and Lindsey Graham in the 2016 elections.[22]

George Soros plays his game well above the level of Republican vs Democrat. Do not underestimate the impact of his financial support. He is a globalist that is attempting to rule America. He has spent $Billions in attempting to transform this country (and the world) to his vision.[23] He believes he is smarter than you, more powerful than you, and more important than you.

Two things he doesn't have, however, are your voice and your vote. If you understand the game that he and the Ruling Class Oligarchs are playing, you can thwart them. Later in this book we will discuss specifically how *you* can make a difference, but for now ask yourself... Are you willing to be a superhero? StressFreeBill believes that *everyone* who stands up to the self-appointed Ruling Class is, indeed, a superhero. Let that thought roll around in your head for a while; try it on for size. The next time you sign your name, add a *007* at the end of it... See what it feels like.

The Founding Fathers pledged their lives, their fortunes, and their sacred honor... All *we* need do is pay attention and not close our eyes to what's happening around us. I'm in... How about you?

CHAPTER ELEVEN

Ruling Class Judiciary

Power Corrupts

Our Founding Fathers were fully aware of this. Most of us tend to forget that civilization had existed on our planet for thousands of years prior to the American Revolution. Humanity had already played around with untold variations of government. Investing power in a single ruler had never worked out well; emperors, dictators, kings and queens... all totalitarians inevitably end up abusing their people. Slightly diffusing that power among a small group of oligarchs (like a politburo or disempowered legislature) also didn't seem to improve things – ask any citizen of a communist, Nazi, socialist, or fascist government.

The inescapable lesson was that Power Corrupts, and Absolute Power Corrupts Absolutely.

Ancient Greece had tried the novel idea of diffusing power throughout the entire citizenry. Every person (excluding women and slaves, of course) had a vote. This worked well for a while and one suspects that its success was aided by the fact that, at least in terms of technology, it was simpler times. Eventually, however, it led to internecine fighting among the Greek city-states of Sparta, Athens, Thebes, and Karen. With no clear leadership, a weakened Greece would eventually fall to the Romans.[1]

This is where the brilliance of our Founding Fathers really shines. Building on the weak example of the House of Commons in Britain, they designed a government that still maintained strong leadership yet diffused the power by separating it into three coequal branches.[2]

This is why the United States government has an Executive Branch, a Legislative Branch, and a Judicial Branch.

The key to making this system work is that the branches are equal but *separate*.

An oversimplified way to explain this is to say that the Legislative Branch (Congress) is in charge of making the laws and authorizing government spending, the Executive Branch (the President) is in charge of national defense as well as executing and enforcing the laws, and the Judicial Branch (federal judges) are in charge of interpreting the laws.

In other words, the President cannot order a federal judge to rule a certain way. Senators and congressmen can pass laws but they cannot throw you in jail if you ignore them. And federal judges cannot tell the President how to defend our country. *But as this book is being written, our Ruling Class Judiciary is trying to do just that.*

Ruling Class Judiciary noun / ruː.lɪŋ ˈklæs ˈjo͞oˈdiSHē ˌerēˌjo͞oˈdiSHərē /
Federal judges that no longer feel constrained to simply interpreting the US Constitution or Congressional Legislation. Through an ever-expanding doctrine of Judicial Activism, they are convinced they have a duty to *guide* our country to a superior vision of the way things *should* be. They validate their usurpation of power by claiming the U.S. Constitution to be a Living Document. A document that must be modified and reinterpreted to fit modern times. And, of course, *they* are the only ones fit to determine that reinterpretation.

The clear *Separation of Powers* defined by our three branches of government is designed to give us a system of *Checks and Balances*. The idea being if any one branch of the government oversteps its authority or attempts to usurp the power of another branch, the other two branches can gang up to stop it. *But what if one (or both) of the other two branches don't want it stopped?*

This, unfortunately, is the current state of affairs we find in the United States of America. The Ruling Class Intelligentsia that has indoctrinated and educated our judiciary for generations belongs to the same culture that spawns our Ruling Class Politicians. Both the Judicial and legislative branches of our current government are literally on the same page; they are overseeing the rights of *We the People* being evermore passed into the hands of the Ruling Class. Congress continues to legislate away our rights to privacy and property while judges reinterpret the Constitution to allow it. Indeed, prior to the election of President Donald Trump it could be argued that for a number of terms the Executive Branch has also been populated by Ruling Class Politicians derived from this Ruling Class Culture.

StressFreeBill is not by nature a pessimistic person. But as we begin to realize how thoroughly all three branches of government have been corrupted by this Ruling Class culture, it becomes ever more obvious that the time to act is now. I do believe with all my being that there is still time to work within the system, within the law, to fight the good fight, regain our country, and once again start educating our children in the truths and values that made America great. We will discuss specific calls to action in a later chapter, but I charge every reader to consider the following question... *What are you willing to do, within the law, to preserve and protect the United States of America and all she stands for?*

CHAPTER TWELVE

The Ruling Class Bureaucracy

What Is the Deep State?

Most of us have heard pundits and journalists talk about the Deep State. We watch almost daily as the Washington Post or New York Times publishes some shocking bit of 'news' about President Donald Trump – and the origin of these 'credible leaks' is always some un-named source from the White House, the Intelligence Community, or the Office of the Special Counsel.

Setting aside for the moment that many of these leakers are committing felonies,[1] [2] and that felons aren't generally considered credible, the entire Ruling Class Media then spends the next day or week discussing how damaging these unfounded revelations are and how dire the situation is for our President. And even though a good many of these leaks are ultimately proven entirely false, the Ruling Class Media eagerly awaits the next leak and the frenzy starts all over again. This happens over and over; you can set your watch by it.

This is where the term 'Deep State' comes in. These leakers are supposedly life-long non-partisan government employees deeply embedded in the bureaucracies of Washington who reportedly fear greatly for the course of our nation and feel compelled to get the word out about the democracy-threatening atrocities being committed by the Trump Administration.

But is that true?

Let's look at a far more likely scenario – but first, we need to make a quick review of how our Federal Bureaucracies work…

We have previously discussed our three separate but coequal branches of government (Executive, Legislative, and Judicial). This is the doctrine of Separation of Powers and is intended to provide checks and balances against any one branch getting out of control.

The Executive Branch (the President) has the Constitutional authority to execute and enforce the law and protect the nation, among other things. He does this by presiding over massive federal police and defense organizations such as the FBI, CIA, NSA, Homeland Security as well as the Department of Defense.

In addition, the President also oversees vast numbers of civil servants divided up among the various departments such as Treasury, the State Department, Health and Human Services, etc.

There are almost 22 million people employed by federal, state, and local government in the United States.[3] That's almost as many people as *all* the Fortune 500 companies employ *combined.*[4] It is almost double the number of people employed in manufacturing positions nationwide.[3] Even if you remove the 1.4 million military personnel that still leaves a staggering number of people whose salaries are being paid by the taxpayer. Of these, 2.79 million are federal civil servants[5] of which slightly over 4,100 are political appointees.[6] [7]

One quick side note: The Ruling Class Media and Ruling Class Politicians have been trying to claim that the size (in employees) of the Federal government has been remaining steady or declining.[8] [9] This is a great example of how they try to manipulate and mislead *We the People*. Many of this number of ever-increasing positions have been pushed into contractor status. So, while they are technically not *employees*, they are still paid with our tax dollars and are doing the same job.[10] The Federal workforce *is* expanding.

The 4,100 political appointees make up the department heads, managers, assistant directors, and other top-level positions among the various agencies. Typically many (almost all) are replaced every time a new President takes office. This is common sense – a new administration wants its own people that believe in its own agenda running things.

It is impossible for any new incoming administration to have all 4,100 political appointees interviewed and lined up on day one of their administration. Therefore many of these positions remain occupied by the previous administration's appointees until they are replaced. Typically, new administrations start by replacing the top positions, like cabinet secretaries and agency directors, first. This allows those that will be in charge to help in the selection of other appointed personnel that will fill out their departments.

Every administration wants their own appointees in office as quickly as possible, but it has never before been considered an issue of national security because it is always assumed that the political appointees of any administration will place country before politics.

But what if that were no longer true? What if a vast number of political appointees no longer value America over and above their own agenda?

> **Ruling Class Bureaucracy** noun / ru:.lɪŋ 'klæs 'byoo͞ räkrəsē /
> Career and politically appointed bureaucrats that do not believe in American Exceptionalism. They have their own agenda for the course of America and arrogantly believe they have a moral imperative to enact their 'smarter vision.' They show no regard for the will of the people and will engage in subversive, illegal and immoral acts to further their own egos and agenda. To these people, patriotism is naïve and the provenance of fools.

The Obama administration gained a reputation for staffing the government agencies and departments with ideological zealots. For example, John Brennan (formally the Director of the CIA) has a well-documented history of promoting gay rights.[11] [12] [13] StressFreeBill actually watched a credible guest on Fox News accuse Brennan of purposely jamming as many gays as possible onto the employment rolls of the CIA regardless of an individual's competence or if they were the best qualified to do the job. That pundit has certainly not been the only one to question Brennan's integrity in this respect.[13]

Let's be clear, Obama apologists will be quick to accuse StressFreeBill of being homophobic or anti-gay or whatever the popular putdown of the moment happens to be... The truth is, I couldn't care less about someone's sexual preference, skin color, gender, religion, or what color of toothbrush they use. I care about the United States of America and for those that serve her to do so well. I care that *our country* be our civil servants' top agenda. I do not care if John Brennan is gay or whether he hired gay people to serve in the CIA; I care that he reportedly stuffed as many ideological zealots as possible into the CIA and that those zealots place their own agenda ahead of the Constitution of the United States, the Rule of Law, and the expressed will of *We the People* (the election results). I would feel the same way if his agenda was to stuff white people, women, or Hindus into the agency at the expense of competence or loyalty to America.

Remember also that these appointees typically represent the top levels of the department. After eight years of being in charge, what are the odds that ideological zealots will promote civil servants with the same philosophies and repress the careers of those that believe differently?

Also, realize that we have good documentation about John Brennan and his self-admitted LGBT agenda at the CIA... But what about the Justice Department? Or, the State Department? Does anyone really believe that the Obama administration didn't encourage this type of ideological prioritizing in all of the federal departments and agencies that fall under the purview of the Executive Branch?

If we have a new President, why doesn't he simply replace all of the Obama appointments?

Well, that's the plan. But it can't be done overnight even under the best of circumstances... And our current situation is *anything but* the best of circumstances.

Of the 4,100 positions needing appointments, 1,242 of them need Senate confirmation.[7] And remember, most of these represent the top bosses in the various departments. Most of them need to be appointed first, before the thousands of other political appointees can be replaced.

And herein lies the problem...

Chuck Schumer, the Senior Democrat in the United States Senate, vowed to slow-walk Senate approval of Trump administration appointees.[14] [15] He has been largely successful in this; the last member of President Trump's 15-member cabinet was only approved by the Senate in April of 2017 – three full months after the new administration took office.[16] *It took three months to appoint just 15 people!*

Before we start thinking this is simply a partisan Republican vs Democrat issue, we should remember that the Republicans control the Senate. So, how can Senator Schumer slow down anything?

Because Ruling Class Politicians, both Democrat *and Republican*, don't want the process speeded up...

They do not want the advances of the globalist agenda rolled back, and stopping such a rollback is a much higher priority than any partisan squabbling. So, Ruling Class Politicians of both parties prefer to stall and resist. To them, every roadblock and impediment imaginable must be thrown up against the current administration.

In a previous chapter we talked about the Byrd Rule – a Byzantine Senate Rule whose only valid purpose is to give cover to politicians not wanting to respond to the *Will of the People*. Another Senate Rule allows two days of debate before a motion to force cloture — a measure to end debate before a vote. The same rule then gives an additional 30 hours of debate before a vote can take place (to stall even longer, the democrats will many times then boycott confirmation hearings to prevent the required quorum). At the current historically slow rate of confirmations, it will be impossible for the Senate to confirm all of the Trump Administration nominations before the end of his first four-year term. The Republican Senate leader, Mitch McConnell, could call a simple majority vote to revise or suspend these rules at any time... *But he doesn't choose to do so. Instead, he allows the*

Democrats to drastically hamper President Trump's ability to build a government.

StressFreeBill would suggest that if any readers are still harboring doubt that there is a self-appointed Ruling Class in Washington that spans and supersedes both political parties, this example alone should put that thought to rest.

As we shall talk about in a later chapter, the Obama administration made a number of questionable, probably unethical, and definitely unprecedented moves right before leaving office. An important one that helps explain how we end up with a Ruling Class Bureaucracy has to do with the transition of political appointees to federal civil servant jobs. In other words, in the weeks and months before the Obama administration left office many political appointees applied to have their status changed from *appointee* to *employee*. Because of a lackadaisical approach to federal guidelines and reporting, no one knows for sure how many political appointees actually tried to do this – we only know that it was well over 100 and at least 88 were successful.[17] [18]

It should also be noted that besides hiding ideological partisans within the bureaucracy, that strategy makes them almost impossible to get rid of once discovered. Because of Public Sector Unions and Civil Service regulations, it is almost impossible to fire a federal civil service worker.[19] This is why an employee of the EPA only received a 30-day suspension after being *convicted* of stealing thousands of dollars' worth of government equipment.[20] This is also why it is taking almost a year to take any disciplinary action against the Veterans Administration nurse that was caught operating on a veteran *while intoxicated.*[19]

The effect of all this skullduggery is to bestow upon President Trump a government that opposes him. Honest people may disagree over the motives outlined here, but the behavior and effects are documented facts. Remember, *Behavior Never Lies.*

Once again, StressFreeBill wants to emphasize that this is not about politics as we know it... President Donald Trump represents the duly elected *Will of the People*. The agendas he is attempting to enact are the agendas of *the People*. The *resistance* buried deep within the federal bureaucracy is not anti-Republican; it is anti-democracy. It is anti-Constitutional. And the felonious lengths the Ruling Class Bureaucracy is willing to go to undermine and subvert the ability of this administration to govern proves them to be anti-American.

CHAPTER THIRTEEN

Ruling Class Suck-ups

StressFreeBill took drama classes in high school and college (I was also in the band, lettered in football, and was on the school chess team – I know, I was a weird kid). None of that means anything, of course, except to say that anyone who doesn't believe certain personality types are attracted to specific professions or organizations didn't have the same experiences I did.

Generalizations can be dangerous. Not all geniuses are socially inept, for example. But stereotypes, on the other hand, can be useful. Stereotypes can describe trends and tendencies or simply point out statistical anomalies in demographic groups. In other words, no matter what the PC Police try to claim, a stereotype is a comment on the group, never the individual.

Throughout my lifetime, Hollywood has always had an ideological tendency to lean to the left. Over the last decade, however, either the percentage of liberals in the entertainment industry has increased dramatically, or their effectiveness in *shouting down* and silencing conservative voices has increased dramatically. Probably both. There is no longer even any pretense of respecting other people's opinions; their groupthink is their *truth*. And they will mercilessly mock and laugh at anyone not smart enough or cool enough to believe in that truth.

Doesn't that remind you of the *cool kids* in high school?

The movie industry always stereotypes *the cool kids in high school*. Claire, Molly Ringwald's character in The Breakfast Club, and the movie Mean Girls starring Lindsay Lohan are good examples. These groups are always portrayed as being made up of rich stuck-up snobs that are only popular because of their looks and money. And, of course, everybody else wants what they have, *popularity*. Some other kids want to be popular so much that they will do anything to be accepted into this group. What's important to understand here is that the liberals in Hollywood are generalizing this stereotype – *they actually believe that **all** the cool kids they ever knew are like this.*

They don't know any better because again, in my experience, most of them were never a part of that Cool Kids group. But just like Lindsay Lohan's character, *they always wanted to be...*

Well, now *they* are the celebrities. Everyone wants to take their picture and know the intimate details of their life. Everyone wants to be just like them... Now *they* are the cool kids. *And they're acting out the stereotype of the way they think Cool Kids act!* Snobbishness, elitism, and barely concealed disdain for *the little people* are the Cool Kids role they play in real life. The irony of the entire situation is that these people have never grown past desperately wanting to be accepted. And now that they're celebrities, they realize the group they *really* want to be accepted into is the Ruling Class – the political, intellectual, and economic movers and shakers of their culture. Their motivation for political activism isn't stemming from closely held beliefs; it comes from a deep-seated desire to *belong*. This is the reason their knowledge of the issues is typically so shallow; they are simply emulating the behavior of the group they want to be accepted into.

So, does StressFreeBill have some advanced degree in sociology that he hasn't told anyone about? No, but for a businessperson that's built organizations of tens of thousands of people a certain amount of understanding and insight regarding social dynamics has proven important. And actually, I'm saying most of this tongue-in-cheek anyway; even I find it hard to believe this group's behavioral motivations can be so simplistic...

I certainly don't want to be guilty of generalizing, and I cannot claim to know what's in the heart of people I otherwise enjoy watching sing beautiful songs, perform athletic feats, or through their acting ability take me to new levels of imagination and entertainment. I can, however, analyze their behavior and fit it to a model that makes sense to me. And the model is laughingly familiar...

What's not funny, however, is the effect this psychosis is having on our society. One only has to watch a single episode of The View to be shocked by the political ignorance expressed. StressFreeBill has no problem with someone espousing a different political view... But if you're going to do it on national television could you at least do it with some coherence? Is it too much to ask for that you be able to articulate and explain your opinions? There seems to be an arrogant assumption that because people want your autograph they will also automatically adopt your views – no explanation necessary.

This mindset allows these people to be easily manipulated. Most of this group did not gain their wealth via extreme intelligence, advanced education, or from building businesses that have employed thousands and benefited millions. There is residual guilt here and a lingering sense of subliminal inferiority. In other words, when exposed to members of the Ruling Class Oligarchy, the Ruling Class Intelligentsia, and Ruling Class Politicians... *They still want to belong.*

We call these people, Ruling Class Suck-ups.

> **Ruling Class Suck-ups** noun / ruː.lɪŋ ˈklæs ˈsuhk uhps/
> Celebrities with outspoken and shallow political views that are contrary to Free Speech, The Rule of Law, and American Patriotism. They use their celebrity status not to debate issues, but to mock and ridicule those that believe differently.

That may sound rather harsh, and I want to emphasize that it certainly doesn't apply to every celebrity. But regardless of whether the Ruling Class

Suck-ups are being manipulated or if we wind up discovering they are the genius masterminds behind the entire globalist movement, they are promoting the subversion of our duly elected government. They are attempting to delegitimize and undermine the Rule of Law and the Constitution of the United States. Through their spew of hateful rhetoric and intolerance they, along with their allies in the Ruling Class Media, are radicalizing a lesser informed element of our society. A radicalization that will ultimately, and assuredly, lead to violence.

StressFreeBill will discuss in a later chapter effective methods for countering the influence of the Ruling Class Suck-ups. But make no mistake, unless we want to see our country unalterably changed, we must stand up to them.

As a final note and for what it's worth, in my experience and research the *cool kids* clique found in most high schools has its share of rich arrogant and stuck up beautiful people, but it also includes a large number of genuinely nice attractive and/or talented kids whose aloofness arises not from arrogance, but simply a lack of common interest with those that spend their days gossiping and running down others. And for the record, StressFreeBill never quite managed to attain the *Cool Kid* status at his high school. Oh well...

CHAPTER FOURTEEN

Socialism vs Capitalism

StressFreeBill likes to keep things very simple. When first deciding to write this book, there was a choice to make. Make it erudite and sophisticated, highly technical, and use a vocabulary and sentence structure that would appeal to the academics and critics... Or, write it in the best way to get the point across.

This doesn't mean dumbing things down. I highly suspect the readers of this book will carry a higher than average IQ. But there is a tendency in journalism, in the media, and in our society at large to sometimes speak obliquely. There is also a tendency for authors, pundits, etc. to be a little vague at times in order to avoid being proven completely wrong in the course of events.

I've never been much like that.

And although being that straightforward can sometimes be a little awkward and definitely not the smartest approach to every situation, it has sometimes blessed me with clarity. So, while on occasion I might *mention* that I am oversimplifying an explanation for purposes of understanding, there are other times I just don't bother – I just want to get to the point. It is these *other times,* however, that academics, critics and opponents can pick apart and use to trash an author.

This discussion of Socialism and Capitalism will give them such an opening...

Any discussion about philosophies of government can be as deep as one wishes to make it, but there is no good reason for this to be a long chapter. These are simple concepts, and for our purposes I'm going to stick to the essence of what socialism and capitalism actually are. And it *is* important that we briefly refresh our memory on the fundamental differences of each. After all, the globalists and the left keep pushing us ever further into the realms of socialism.

Socialism is just a watered-down form of communism.

The concept of communism is simple and beautiful: *From each according to their ability; To each according to their needs.* [1]

In other words, a big strong man can plow a field faster and grow more grain than a small weak man (or woman). So, according to communism, we should take the extra grain grown by the strong man and redistribute part of it to the weak man. This ensures that each man has an equal amount of grain.

The whole idea of communism is supposedly based on the concept of *fairness.*

But there's a problem with this... Mainly, it's that *Life Isn't Fair.* Throughout human history, every single time this type of government has been attempted it has failed miserably.[2] This is where our friends on the left start screaming, "Wait a minute! China is communist and it hasn't failed!" They are almost right...

The disparity of income and standard of living between the rural and urban populations in China is a ticking time bomb, and this rising social and economic pressure has only been slightly ameliorated by introducing capitalistic market forces into their economy.[3] In other words, to survive, China's economy is becoming more capitalist and less communistic with every passing year (which is one of the reasons China *will not* get into a trade war with us – but that is a different subject altogether).[3] More importantly, the Chinese government maintains power not by the consent of the governed, but rules by force. Only extreme crazies openly advocate for that (unless, of course, they see themselves as the rulers). Much the same can be said about North Vietnam and North Korea – communist client states still propped up by China but doomed to fail. Communism is a demonstrably failed concept.[4]

Socialism is more subtle, but still doomed to fail. It is doomed because its central premise – that government can make life fair for everyone – is absolutely false.

Modern examples would include Greece, Brazil, and Venezuela. They always fail because inevitably the strong man gets tired of working harder than everyone else for the same amount of grain, and the weak man realizes there's no need to push himself to work hard at all... After all, he's going to get the same amount of grain no matter how much (or how little) he produces.

Communism and socialism are beautiful ideas; they just don't work.

So, if these philosophies of government never work why are they attempted over and over again, century after century, throughout human history? Two reasons...

First, you can always find people stupid enough and egotistical enough to think that if they were just in charge *they* could make it work...

Secondly, most of the people (typically revolutionaries) that advocate this type of philosophy *already know* it won't work... *It's just something that sounds good that they can sell to 'the people' so that in turn 'the people' will give them power...* It's an easy sell to the less accomplished in our society; there will always be people willing to buy into *Class Envy*.

Remember this when we get to the later chapters discussing how the Ruling Class manages to co-opt its different ideological factions into one seamless culture..

Under communism, the government owns everything... the field, the grain, even the farmhouse you live in. Under socialism, you can own the field, the grain, and even the farmhouse... But the government is still going to come in and take part of your harvest and redistribute it to those they consider deserving. And, oh by the way... *They* get to decide who is deserving.

Yes, every form of government needs to take some of your grain (assess taxes) in order to function. But a socialistic government taxes the rich man at a higher rate (the strong man), the average man at a lower rate (the weak man), and gives money to the poor (the non-working man). The more socialistic the government, the higher they tax the rich and the more they give to the poor.

This is called, *Redistribution of Wealth.*

You might be thinking that this sounds an awful lot like the US Tax Code... And you'd be right. An income tax that taxes you a higher *percentage* the more you make is called a Progressive Tax. Just like the left in our country and the Democrats call themselves the Progressive party. An easy way to remember this is to understand that Progressive means they are *progressing towards socialism.*

StressFreeBill believes with all his heart that Income Tax is evil. *Any* tax on income is evil. It makes much more sense to tax people when they spend money, not when they earn it. It doesn't take a lot of smarts to understand that you should reward the things you want more of and not reward the things you want less of. As a society we should be rewarding the activity we want (like hard work, competence, good luck, and success), and not rewarding the activity we don't want (like sloth, laziness, inability, or just plain bad luck). But this leads us into a conversation about the Fair Tax, and that's a subject for the StressFreeBill.com website...[5]

Suffice it to say that we already have many aspects of socialism present in the United States of America. Fortunately, we are still mainly a capitalistic society.

Capitalism is the engine that drives innovation, success, hard work, risk-taking, and breakthrough technologies.

Capitalism is the opposite of communism or socialism. It allows people to keep the fruits of their own labor and therefore gives people incentive to be successful. Capitalism is what gave the pioneers and immigrants to our country the incentive and ability to become the most successful and richest country in the world. It is what allowed us to distribute our innovation and technology to others and increase the standard of living for the billions that live in other countries. When the government simply *gets out of the way* and allows people to reap the rewards of their own labor anything is possible. *In other words, everyone grows as much grain as possible because it's in their best interest to do so.*

Capitalism is the meaning behind the phrase, *A Rising Tide Lifts All Boats...* [6]

Contrary to what progressives and socialists will tell you, the United States is also one of the most compassionate and definitely the most generous country in the world.[7] [8] Socialism *forces* people to give to the poor; capitalism *allows* people to give to the poor. Compassion cannot be forced or it will be retarded.[9]

It is important that we have this quick review because we all need to decide which kind of world we want to live in. The push for globalism is very real; but the current push is for global socialism. For most of the last 200 years the United States has been a shining example of what other countries should strive for. Many of the new democracies in Latin America, for example, have patterned their Constitutions after ours.[10] Our culture of freedom, hard work, honesty, integrity and especially the rule of law serves as an example of how countries should develop their societies and their economies. Because of the example of the United States of America, more countries than ever before have liberated their populations, improved their standard of living, increased education and opportunity for their people, and embraced ideas of human dignity and freedom.

None of this would be possible with socialism. Under global socialism all of the great examples that spur humanity to greater heights will wither. StressFreeBill strongly believes that the best way for the United States to help the billions of other people on this planet is to show the way, set the example, and lead the world toward prosperity and wow the world with our compassionate generosity... Not by forced redistribution of our wealth and sovereignty to the point where all countries are equal.

That would be fair... It would also be tragic.

CHAPTER FIFTEEN

Climate Change

StressFreeBill considers himself a scientist.

Certainly not by occupation but, rather, by vocation. I understand the scientific method and am comfortable reading peer-reviewed research, particularly in the world of medicine. And while I would certainly not claim to have the depth of knowledge of a medical doctor or other PhDs, my decades of owning businesses that worked closely with such individuals, as well as my personal fascination and interest in all things science, have given me a good understanding of how to view the physical world around us.

Because I also understand the world of business and marketing I have, perhaps, an uncommon advantage when looking at the subject of climate change. I have some insight into motivations and human nature that perhaps allows me to know this is more than just about science...

My purpose in this chapter is not to debunk the issue of anthropogenic (man-made) climate change so much as it is to explain how the issue is being used by globalists to denude the sovereignty of the United States of America. This is not to say that I'm going to shy away from the subject; I'm just not going to spend a bunch of pages on it here. There are four reasons for this: 1) We have now had generations of Americans indoctrinated via the educational system to believe in it, 2) Therefore, most of those former students have already made up their minds on the issue, 3) Most of those very same students have no idea what the scientific method is and would not be swayed by a scientific argument, and 4) I'm tired of trying and it doesn't really make a difference when it comes to understanding what's happening in our country politically.

Having said that, let me spend one short paragraph summing up my belief and giving a brief explanation...

Climate change is real; the climate is constantly changing... always has, always will. The activities of man *certainly* contribute to climate change; it is said the flapping of a butterfly's wings in China is able to cause a hurricane in the Caribbean... Everything is connected and everything has an effect. *How much* is man affecting the change in climate? *No one knows*, but probably not very much.

What I just stated are actual facts. Pretty much anything else you hear *on either side of the issue* that claims to be authoritative is simply propaganda.

The argument for man-made climate change is based on scientific models. All the 'evidence' you hear discussed in the Ruling Class Media are either the data that goes into the models or the predictions that come out of the models. Data can be manipulated and scientific models are nothing other than *educated guesses*.

The scientific world is divided up into the hard sciences and the soft. The hard sciences (physics, mathematics, etc.) deal with scientific models that produce results that can be predicted *and* consistently duplicated by others. Hard science deals with *verifiable* outcomes we call proofs. The soft sciences deal with scientific models that predict results that *cannot* be confirmed or consistently duplicated. Climate science falls firmly into this category. So does polling science.

Every election cycle polling companies use scientific algorithms and formulas to predict the outcome of elections. They poll segments of the population for data, plug it into their model, and make a prediction. This is valid science, but it is *soft* science.

And it is often wrong.[1] [2]

And it is sometimes right, which shows that polling science can be useful. Climate science models, on the other hand, *are almost never right*.[3] This is certainly because climate science is *much* more complicated. Whereas pollsters only need to collect data from a few hundred to a few thousand individuals, climate scientists need millions of points of data. Good climate models require data such as ground temperatures at numerous worldwide locations and a variety of topographies at various times of the day and year; ditto for wind velocities and ocean currents, etc.[4] It is complicated further by the fact that these data sets are worthless unless the *exact* same readings are available for every year going back as long as possible (preferably centuries or longer). It is almost impossible to get accurate data, let alone get accurate predictions. Yet we have been teaching our children and believing Ruling Class Politicians when they say it is *settled science*. Why?

Because there is an agenda. Actually, there are a lot of agendas. Remember, StressFreeBill likes to look at behavior, not rhetoric. One behavior that is extremely concerning is the avalanche of false and altered data being plugged into the models in the first place.[5] Also concerning are the plethora of models that do not include or disproportionately discount factors such as ocean currents and solar storms.[6] These factors, especially solar storms (sunspots), are known to have major impact on global temperature.[7] And unbelievably, many so-called climate scientists refuse to even acknowledge the clear data showing a 20-year pause in the rise of global temperatures (most probably because their models don't predict it).[8] [9]

All of this out-of-character and *seriously* unprofessional behavior by a concentrated and vocal minority of the scientific community leads StressFreeBill to conclude there are hidden forces and hidden agendas at play. This is a reasonable conclusion based on observation.

But what are the agendas?

I think it is easier to understand why Ruling Class Politicians, Ruling Class Media, and Ruling Class Oligarchs would want to push the idea of man-made climate change, so we'll address that last. What's seemingly harder to explain is why any type of scientist, hard or soft, would falsify data, leave out data, and/or totally abandon the scientific method? It's harder to understand, that is, until we remember Galileo.

In 1633, the now famous astronomer Galileo Galilei was convicted of heresy.[10] His published works were prohibited and he spent the rest of his life confined to house arrest. His crime? Suggesting that the earth was not the center of the universe; instead suggesting that the earth actually orbited around the sun.

Galileo was neither the first nor the last scientist to be persecuted by governing authority. Even Albert Einstein suffered persecution at the hands of the German government and suffered loss of all titles and privilege there.[11]

We must remember that scientists are typically of the intelligentsia. And the intelligentsia survives now, as it did in Galileo's time, at the suffrage of the Ruling Class. There has always been pressure on scientists to validate existing modes of thought, be they theological or ideological. Historically, a fair number of scientists have been of high character and resisted; many have not. As will become obvious, there has perhaps never been a time in human history when more pressure has been placed upon scientists to validate a preconceived outcome. Anthropogenic Climate Change itself has become a religion.[12] Grant money, social acceptance, the ability to publish, even the opportunity to make a living are at stake for the vast majority of legitimate scientists who wish to study the Earth's climate.

Make no mistake; there are many fanatical believers when it comes to anthropogenic climate change. You can find them in all of the self-appointed Ruling Classes, but especially the Ruling Class Media and Ruling Class Suck-ups. Conversely, there are exceptions. By observing behavior StressFreeBill has come to believe that most in the Ruling Class Oligarchy are not true believers. Or, maybe more accurately, they couldn't care less...

The religion of Climate Change is being used as a hammer to break down the sovereignty of the United States of America and other Western nations.[13] It is the perfect excuse for globalist to claim that no one country should be allowed to be more industrious, more ambitious, and therefore more rich than other countries. International agreements like the proposed Paris Climate Accords did not restrict carbon emissions from all countries (as most people think). It only proposed restricting them for advanced Western countries – primarily the United States. The biggest polluters, countries like China, Russia, and almost the entire Third World would be free to actually *increase* their carbon emissions for a large number of years in order to give them the chance to industrially *catch up* with the United States. At which point (theoretically), and over a decade in the future, they would start reducing their own emissions.[14]

The Paris climate Accords had *nothing* to do with climate change or benefiting the planet; it had everything to do with the globalist goal of leveling the international playing field, removing American sovereignty, and redistributing the industrial and technological wealth of the world.

The Paris Climate Accords were to be the culmination and pinnacle achievement of the entire Climate Change movement. For those of us that study behavior, however, it serves as a microcosm exposing the true agenda behind the movement.

StressFreeBill has compassion for the tens of millions of people around the globe that have been duped into supporting this hidden agenda under what are probably false pretenses. However, it does not change the fact that this movement is a weapon being used against us. We must resist it. We must stand up to it with compassion but firm resolve. I will always be open to valid new evidence about the climate and this planet we live on (I was a *conservationist* before anyone knew what an *environmentalist* was). But at this point in time, there is more valid reason to worry about an asteroid impacting the planet than there is to worry about man affecting global temperatures.

And all of *those* risks pale in comparison to the risk of global socialism.

CHAPTER SIXTEEN

Globalism vs Nationalism

StressFreeBill grew up in the era of Star Trek. Watching the show it was obvious that their society had advanced far beyond ours. For example, the earth no longer used money and the planet was united with a central government. Indeed, the name *United Federation of Planets* implied that this government spanned more than just earth.

Those altruistic dreams of a somewhat utopian fictional future inspired more than one generation to dream big about our own destiny – and some of us never stopped. After a long business career, I now write science fiction novels under a different pen name (William Lee Gordon). Like all good writers I was inspired by events from my past... And that vision of what humanity could achieve has never left me.

Unfortunately, reality seems to follow more along the Star Wars theme. The Evil Empire is, well... evil. The Emperor and his cronies want to control everything and everyone. The heroes are the freedom loving rebels that just want to be left alone with their families to build their future.

StressFreeBill is on record as stating he believes that eventually Earth *will* have a global government. It won't happen tomorrow, but it *will* eventually come about. The issue at stake is what kind of government will it be? If we want the future to be a place where all people benefit from technology, where everyone has high quality health care and education, where every child has the freedom to follow any path and find their own destiny... Then shouldn't we be applying the forms of government that have proven to take us that direction, rather than trying to emulate the types of government that have led to poverty, despair, enslavement, and misery?

I've said it before and I'll say it again... I don't care if we have a global government, as long as it's *our* government.

As evidenced throughout this book, the international push to globalism is very real. But we must understand the means and the motives of that push. Multinational Corporations and the Ruling Class Oligarchs that run many of them wish to develop emerging markets. Like all businesses they want to expand, and to do that they need new customers. Many of these potential new markets, however, are found in underdeveloped countries. Countries with massive poverty. The challenge for the multinationals is that an impoverished population cannot afford to purchase televisions, automobiles, smart phones, cable TV subscriptions, and any of another thousand commodities offered in the modern world. Most of these Third World countries, at least the ones that have thrown off the yoke of dictators, communism, and socialism, are progressing and their populations are slowly but surely becoming richer. They are slowly but surely finding a better quality of life and a better standard of living. But it's not always happening fast enough for CEOs to satisfy shareholder demands for increased profits.

The faster solution of the Ruling Class Globalists is to redistribute the wealth of the planet.

The United States is a rich country and, compared to most of the world, has a rich population. Rather than holding up that example and encouraging the rest of the world to follow the same model, they scheme to take wealth from the American people and redistribute it among poor countries. They do this by taking jobs (traditionally it's been manufacturing jobs) from America and placing them in those emerging markets.[1] This has multiple benefits for the multinationals; not only can they manufacture their products much less expensively (labor is much cheaper there), but they are in effect taking the US dollars you use to purchase a product and transferring them via wages to the economy of a Third World country. This helps develop that country and enrich the population sufficiently that they can afford to buy products from the multinational.[2] Unfortunately, it takes those dollars out of *our* economy and reduces growth and promotes stagnation here. The best example of this is NAFTA (the North American Free Trade Agreement).[3] This trade agreement has transformed Mexico's economy and increased the profits of a lot of large corporations, but devastated America's middle class.[4]

Based on those profit gorged results from dealing with Mexico, those newly enriched multinationals set their sights on doing what they do best – expanding. Other large corporations have taken notice and want their own multinational opportunity.[5] It has taken years to negotiate with all the individual countries, but in the end it wasn't hard to find willing trade partners in the Pacific Rim that would gladly accept a massive transfer of wealth and jobs from the United States. And because they have already seduced a large number of Ruling Class Politicians, the Ruling Class Oligarchy was quite confident in its ability to ratify the Trans-Pacific Partnership Agreement (TPP). This was a trade agreement between as many as 18 countries that would all but dissolve certain sovereignties held by the United States.[6] Massive amounts of US trade policy would then be controlled by international panels – the globalist dream of breaking down the sovereignty of those pesky nationalist countries (especially the United States) was taking hold.[7]

And then along came President Donald Trump. He declared that the United States would be withdrawing from TPP. As the American economy is the keystone partner in the agreement (or victim, depending on your point of view) this withdrawal all but assures it will never be ratified. Billions of dollars were spent by international Ruling Class Oligarchs in anticipation of the ratification.[8] They can't be happy...[9]

We'll talk more about the effect of Donald Trump winning the election in a later chapter, but to understand the globalist movement we need to realize that this massive transfer of wealth and jobs from the United States has been going on for *decades*. As frantic as they are to correct the *Trump Interruption* of this agenda, they will ultimately look at it as only temporary. The Ruling Class Oligarchs were all but certain of ultimate victory and will not let this pause in fulfilling their agenda derail their plans. And while StressFreeBill readily admits that this is of necessity a somewhat oversimplified explanation, it is important that *We the People* use this pause to assess the situation. The results of this massive move towards globalism are what are important to look at – and the results are that the manufacturing base in America has been gutted.[10] And what was once the healthiest middle class in the world is now enduring the lowest Labor Participation Rate since 1977.[11] And as bad for America as this is, it pales in comparison to what our future holds if we continue down this path...

Manufacturing jobs were the first target of this movement because they traditionally required a less sophisticated and less educated workforce. Today, however, many impoverished countries are educating a significant number of their populations in high tech skills, specifically coding and software. Few Americans realize how large the outside world actually is... For example, *did you know there are more honor roll students in India than there are **students** in the United States!*[12]

And for the jobs that cannot be exported, many companies are now importing the workers. This is where the infamous H-1B visas come into play. Although there is some justified need for farmers and companies to import special and specific skill sets, there is no question the Ruling Class Oligarchy has coerced Ruling Class Politicians into allowing massive abuse of this program.[13] Originally designed to allow the hiring of foreign workers with skills that are simply not available in the American workforce, the H-1B visa program is now being used to replace existing American workers with foreign workers that will willingly work for a much lower salary. This is being done on a massive scale.[14]

Perhaps it's a coincidence, but simultaneously our Ruling Class Intelligentsia has been active in promoting non-STEM (Science, Technology, Engineering, and Mathematics) pursuits for American children.[15] Having a Master's Degree in Women's Studies, Literature, Black History, Journalism, or Social Justice is fine, but it's not going to get you a high-paying job in the STEM sectors (where all the demand is)[16] – especially if you're competing with a recent college graduate from India that will work for one-half to two-thirds of what that same company would have to pay you.

Why would our Ruling Class Intelligentsia want to import so much foreign labor? One reason is that it helps break down the culture. The United States is a country of immigrants, and we have taken in more immigrants and refugees than any other country in the world.[17] As a matter of fact, we were once known as the Melting Pot of the world. That was because when people immigrated here, they *assimilated*. They *wanted* to be a part of our culture; they *wanted* their kids to speak English. Why? Because we were the land of opportunity and like all good parents they wanted better for their children than what they had themselves.

This is again a subject that would require another dedicated book to discuss in full (and is an ongoing discussion on the StressFreeBill.com website), but the current situation our Ruling Classes have maneuvered us into results in *preventing* assimilation. The term *multiculturalism* sounds all nice and pretty until you realize it is the *opposite* of direct assimilation. It can also be at odds with another term – patriotism.

So if we accept the fact that the self-appointed Ruling Classes desire to change the American culture, we have to ask ourselves why...? And what do they want to change it into?

The 'why?' is easy; all politics is downstream from culture. In other words, if you want to move the United States into a political system where power is formally consolidated with the elite (like socialism), you must first undermine the traditions of rugged individualism, personal freedom, and achievement. You must erode the public's belief in *American Exceptionalism* and patriotism.[18] It is far easier to accomplish this with unassimilated immigrants than it is those that were born and raised here. Especially if those numbers include large percentages of poor refugees and illegal immigrants – Remember, these are the groups that *receive* the redistributed wealth under socialism. In other words, promoting Class Warfare is the fastest way to change our culture into accepting and normalizing socialism.

The 'what?' is a little harder to answer... StressFreeBill has not observed a consensus among all the different factions that make up America's self-appointed Ruling Classes. The Ruling Class Intelligentsia definitely favors socialism, but global socialism is simply a means to an end for most of the Ruling Class Oligarchy. We have environmentalists that clamor for a global authority with enough power to force everyone to behave in the eco-friendly ways they dictate, but for most of them that seems to be the beginning and end of their political sophistication. Others like the Ruling Class Media, I'm sure, will be satisfied as long as they and theirs are still recognized as elite and have protected privilege.

Where all these groups are united is in what they *don't* want America to be… They don't want us to be richer than anyone else. They don't want us to be powerful. They don't want us to be independent and they don't want us to lead. Most of all, they don't want us to be that *Shining City upon a Hill* that sets an example for all to follow, and they certainly don't want us holding out a helping hand saying, *"Come on, we'll show you the way…*[19]*"*

It is critically important to understand that, except for the radically hard-core among them, the Ruling Classes don't necessarily *see themselves* as being anti-American. They simply see globalism as a higher form of truth. All those that are cautious of it, including their fellow Americans, are looked at as troglodytes. We are Luddites that are against the advancement of the human race; we are literally not smart enough to see that their view represents inevitable progress and that our cautions are silly and futile gestures. The nuance of *what type* of global cooperation and ultimately what type of global government we should be working for is lost on them.

They view Nationalism in the worst possible terms. What immediately comes to their minds are visions of Hitler's Nationalist Nazi movement. Or the fascism of Mussolini. Or even the nationalist sentiment that led

Europe into World War I. Probably because of their education and indoctrination, they fail to remember that it was American nationalism that saved Europe from themselves in that war. It was that same American nationalism that again saved them (and the world) from the Nazis and fascists in World War II. As a matter of fact, if it wasn't for the sentiment of nationalism America never would have been founded – we never would have revolted against the British. The world owes its riches, its advances, and its entire freedom to the concept of nationalism.

These achievements are the results of *American* nationalism (which is indistinguishable from American Exceptionalism). Contrary to what the Ruling Class Media would have us believe, nationalism is neither good nor evil. Nationalism is about loyalty. The rest of the world has always demanded loyalty to a government; what has made America so unique is that we place our loyalty in an *ideal.*

StressFreeBill is not loyal to the *government* of the United States. StressFreeBill is loyal to the United States of America *'and the Republic for which it stands.'* StressFreeBill will not bow down to any ruler or despotic leader; StressFreeBill *will* place his hand on his heart and pledge allegiance to the concept that every person has an inalienable right to life, liberty, and the pursuit of happiness.

There might be those that argue StressFreeBill is using the term 'Nationalist' incorrectly; that nationalism and patriotism are two totally separate things. I don't want to get into semantics but even if this is true, it would simply be further evidence that the Ruling Class is much better than our side at branding. I do not recall President Trump labeling himself a nationalist; I believe this was a label applied by the Ruling Class Media. But even if he did, there would be no doubt in my mind that he means it the same way I do – as an *America First* patriot. As I will soon explain, I speak Trump. And whether I agree with all of his specific policies or not, he is a champion of *We the People*.

Of course, the Ruling Class will not only deny my conclusions, they will deny the observations themselves. They will refute, deny, rewrite history, and lie about the obvious in order to distort any perception that doesn't fit their narrative.

The Ruling Class will attack what I've said here with ferocity. Remember, to them, all aspects of patriotism and nationalism must be put down, debunked, undermined, and discredited. What cannot be argued with credibility, however, is that StressFreeBill is engaging in hyperbole. This is not some exaggerated rant. As this book evidences, these conclusions are all backed by solid reasoning, sound observation, and valid documentation.

Behavior Never Lies.

Unlike all previous countries in history, Americans do not owe allegiance to our government; our government owes allegiance to *us*. This is the nuance that is misunderstood and ignored by the Ruling Class. Our current government is bloated, inefficient, wasteful, corrupt, and has been weaponized by Ruling

Class Politicians. It is in desperate need of reform. The only hope for our government (and our country) is that *We the People* have the will to take back control.

This is not an impossible mission. It is incumbent upon us to remember that the Ruling Class Oligarchs control the financial puppet strings of everyone else in the Ruling Class. They are not overly concerned about global government; they are concerned with global economics. As long as they can tap into international markets and raise their bottom line they will be happy. Most of them are supporting global socialism (global redistribution of wealth) not out of any ideology or idea of fairness or concern for the poor, but simply as the fastest means to a united global economy where they can operate without impediment.

If the dynamics would change, if redistribution of wealth was no longer the easiest pathway for multinational corporations to expand, many of them would stop supporting socialism. They would stop the financing of mass migration, identity politics, and social disruption. They would withdraw their support of the Ruling Class Intelligentsia, and liberals and environmentalists alike would be left wondering, *'What happened?'* In other words, if the American people stand up and say *'No!'* If we make sure that global socialism is not the path of least resistance, the multinationals will move on... they'll look for another way. They are practical business people, not ideologues. They won't fight to the death over this issue... especially if our government changes the tax code to incentivize them to export products rather than jobs, and negotiates trade deals to give *American companies* the advantage.

We do need to realize that they won't switch gears like this easily. They have invested *decades* into the current strategy and it can't be changed overnight.

What the Ruling Class Media will never tell you is that the Tax Reform and renegotiated Trade Policies of the Trump Administration will accomplish just this. In fact, they will do just the opposite; they will wring their hands and exclaim that it is incomprehensible why the Republicans can't get on the same page to pass tax reform. Make no mistake, the Ruling Class Oligarchs will resist right up until the moment it is no longer in their best interests to do so. There is a long fight ahead of us.

On the StressFreeBill.com website and in a later chapter of this book we will discuss how incredibly easy it's been for the Ruling Class Oligarchy to corrupt, recruit, and seduce Ruling Class Politicians to this globalist open borders mindset. Indeed, in many cases they have found willing accomplices and with the Ruling Class Intelligentsia they have discovered an anti-American pathos that has been easy to co-opt.

When it comes to Globalism vs Nationalism we have to realize that the current driving forces behind globalism have nothing to do with the idealism of Star Trek. At least not on the level of the movers and shakers. StressFreeBill has made it very clear that one axiom he believes in is that *Behavior Never Lies.* Here's another, *Always Follow the Money.* And as we have discussed, there are *trillions* of dollars at stake with the globalist agenda...

CHAPTER SEVENTEEN

Making Sense of it All

In 2015, like many Americans, I was frustrated.

A big part of that frustration was with Congress. Since the elections of November 2014 the Republicans had controlled both houses of Congress yet still weren't getting anything done. Whenever those elected officials were asked about the issues they campaigned on, the inevitable excuse was that even if they passed legislation President Obama wouldn't sign it. To my eyes it seemed as if they were spending more time trying to figure out how to pass an unpopular immigration reform package (the Gang of Eight amnesty) than they were in dealing with the concerns of *We the People*. Quite frankly, I was at the point where I didn't care if the president signed anything or not... I wanted my elected officials to grow a spine and stand up for what (I thought) they believed in.

In 2012 I had watched Mitt Romney totally fumble what I felt was a winnable election. And while Romney was certainly nowhere close to being my ideal candidate, I felt he was closer to my core values than President Obama... Or, so I thought.

I had known for decades that the mainstream media held a liberal bias, but even Fox News (for the most part) seemed to accept without contention that the country was moving leftwards. It left me with a deep sense of sadness and loss.

But there was also a part of me that just didn't believe it. Or, perhaps, I just refused to accept it. I couldn't find it inside myself to really believe much of the country, let alone an overwhelming majority, was moving towards the left... that everyone was starting to believe in redistribution of wealth and socialism as answers to our social ills. *I* didn't feel that way and, while I knew a few others that did, I also knew a whole lot that didn't.

Meanwhile, the Republican Party wasn't giving me much reason for solace. Ever since the election of George H. Bush as president of the United States (following Ronald Reagan), the party had been pushing evermore for larger government. That wasn't the official platform, and no one advocated it when elections would come around, but there was no question that the Republican Party was trending that direction through the candidacies of Bob Dole, John McCain, and Mitt Romney. When George W. Bush gained the presidency, he actually increased the federal budget by a whopping 53%.[1]

StressFreeBill has been accused before of being stubborn, but much of the behavior I was observing in the world around me just didn't make sense. I was starting to realize that something else was going on; that there was more to the story than we were being told. I was missing something from the big picture and

I didn't know what it was. I couldn't yet totally articulate those feelings of mine that would soon turn into an epiphany, but I did make the internal decision to step back, take a deep breath, and look at everything anew.

I very quickly came to several conclusions. The first couple were pretty obvious and were truths I'd known for a while:

We've always known economics is behind all politics, yet it was being discussed less and less by the mainstream media...

James Carville, the Lead Strategist for Bill Clinton's successful 1992 Presidential run, famously kept the staff focused on the message, "The economy, stupid![2]" Another well-known saying is 'the Business of America *is* Business.' Capitalism is the economic system that made this country powerful and great, but can only work in an open and free market. Laissez-faire, the principle of government abstaining from interfering in the workings of the free market, is the principle our economic system is based upon. More and more of network and cable news programming, however, was being geared towards social issues - and typically not just any social issues; the more extreme and inconsequential, seemingly the better. Today, it's gotten to the point where a man being able to use a women's bathroom or how many scoops of ice cream the President takes with his meals literally get far more coverage than the same President signing legislation to roll back the Bureau of Land Management's extensive power grab. If House Joint Resolution 44 (H.J. Res.

44) does get mentioned, it is only in the context of social implications (i.e.: sensationalizing the effects on the environment, the wanton destruction of natural resources, etc.). The huge economic benefit of reopening federal land to responsible oil and natural gas production, commercial fishing, logging, etc. is all but ignored. The jobs and middle-class wealth that will inevitably stem from this rollback are not covered at all.

A long time ago, StressFreeBill used to believe that the media catered to the public interest, that if the media focused more and more on social issues it was because these issues were becoming more and more important to the general public. The 2016 Presidential Election confirmed the long-held suspicion that this is no longer true – and probably hasn't been for a long time. The mainstream media was now squarely in the business of *shaping* public opinion, not catering to it. Whether this was a result of purposeful arrogance, or simply a blindness caused by ideological bias is irrelevant. Whether a shortsighted drive for ratings was the motivation, or whether ratings were just an excuse to implement a preferred ideology is irrelevant. *Behavior never lies*, and regardless of the motivation the results are the same.

Another obvious truth is that in our expanding world US politics can no longer be separated from global politics, yet that same mainstream media has been focusing evermore on relatively parochial issues.

Ask yourself this; except for acts of terrorism and Brexit, what international news are we actually getting from the mainstream media? Prior to Donald Trump making it a campaign issue, did you know *anything* about the mass migration of Muslim immigrants into the European Union and the social unrest it was causing? Again, it might be easy to just assume that the American people aren't that interested in the rest of the world, but think about these newsworthy facts...

The economy of Mexico has benefited greatly since the implementation of NAFTA.[3] Our trade deficit has grown dramatically and billions of dollars now flow out of our country and into theirs every year. Also, did you know that in economic terms, Mexico's largest export is its people? Its largest source of foreign dollars is Remittances. These are the US dollars sent home to families in Mexico by current and former Mexican nationals.[4] The infamous drug cartels of Colombia have, in effect, largely relocated to Mexico and their sales of drugs across the border pull even more dollars out of the US economy.[5] Violence along the Mexican border is at an all-time high and American citizens are being killed.[6] [7]

Every dollar that flows out of the U.S. economy is a dollar that won't be spent here. It won't help create jobs here, and it won't be available for savings and investment. Isn't a journalist's job to report the news and then explain how it impacts all of us?

During a period of recession and the slowest recovery on record, does anyone really believe that these issues might not have *some* interest among the general public? It has been obvious now for decades that the mainstream media has no interest in educating or informing the American people. It has also been very obvious that our intelligentsia has been quick to shout down anyone that even tries to bring up these issues. The politics of personal destruction and accusations of racism and xenophobia are all used to silence anyone trying to expose any international anti-American activity. Regardless of whether you believe this is a result of a coordinated movement, or is simply the side effect of our developing Ruling Class Culture... StressFreeBill stands by his observation that the American people are being shielded from the bigger picture.

Another observation that at first puzzled me was that a large number of CEOs and wunderkind entrepreneurs were supporting the Democrat party with their donations.

There has, of course, always been some of this... But the amounts and ultra-vocal support for the Democrat party was startling – especially from the high-tech sector.[8] It is quite normal for business leaders to 'support' the existing administration. After all, their job is to make nice with Washington, make sure all new regulations for their industry are beneficial to their company, and avoid controversy that might make the stockholders restless or affect the bottom line. It is an open secret among many inside the Beltway and inside the corporate world that the 'shakedown' politicians perpetrate against corporate America is par for the course.[9] But by then the Obama administration was coming to an end. Normally, CEOs would start hedging their bets on which party the next president might be from. For a large corporation to donate to both parties would be a common tactic employed by businesses when approaching an election.[10] It *was* the consensus that Hillary Clinton would be the Democrat nominee but the Republicans hadn't even fielded all of their candidates yet. It struck me as very odd that so many business leaders would so openly declare their support this early in the process.[11] It would be easy to write this off as simply a sea change in the tide of politics, but again it simply felt like there must be more to the story.

One of my most troubling observations, however, had to do with the Republican Party itself.

It was moving further and further away from the things I believe in. StressFreeBill can probably best be ideologically categorized as a Reagan conservative. During the Reagan era there were basically two camps in the Republican Party... There was the Reagan conservative faction, and there were the big business *Country Club* Republicans. This latter group was in many ways polar opposites of the conservatives - especially when it came to the size and power of the federal government. Conservatives believed in reining in the power of the federal government and keeping it as small as possible, the other faction... Not so much.

The thing is, over the intervening decades the term *Conservative* has been morphed out of all recognition. The Country Club Republicans had been aghast at how popular the Reagan ideals were, so they joined the movement – in name only. They appropriated the title *conservative* and started using it for themselves and tutored their young political protégés to always identify themselves with the term. They didn't give up their belief in big government, they simply stole the title. And amazingly, it worked. This big government faction of the Republican Party has for decades now held firm control.[12]

When I started looking at which legislative and gubernatorial Republican candidates these same corporations and the United States Chamber of Commerce supported, it became clear they were all from the 'big government' side of the party. It was also the same large cadre of Republicans that were supportive of increased immigration and amnesty; the group whose advocacy was virtually indistinguishable from open borders.

Another huge red flag was that the Republican Party stopped fighting back.

During the Clinton presidency, Republicans still had some fight in them. They would denounce socialist trending policies, advocate free enterprise and the rule of law, and defend American values. This all came to a screeching halt during the Obama administration.[13] The only attempts Congress made to thwart the blatantly anti-American and socialist policies of President Obama were for show.[14] To any careful observer it was obvious that the Republican leadership in the Senate and House, along with the majority of its party's members, were more interested in their careers than they were in keeping campaign promises or honoring traditional values.

All of these observations along with a hundred others led me to a conclusion… If *We the People* had any hope of gaining back control of our government we needed to find and elect a suicide candidate for the President of the United States.

A Suicide President would be a champion that was willing to commit political suicide if that's what the job required - one that didn't care about making a career in politics. He would be a candidate strong enough not to care about faddish public opinion polls – one that would honor his campaign promises regardless of what the media claimed the people really wanted. He would be a President that would be willing to go into the office knowing his stubborn integrity might prevent him from being reelected to a second term. He would be a man (or woman) that was strong enough to tell the truth and not worry about the consequence. He would be a man who could go in and expose the hypocrisy and duplicity of Washington…

CHAPTER EIGHTEEN

And Along Came Donald J. Trump

StressFreeBill has been calling for a suicide President since at least 2013... And I had no idea I would be talking about Donald J. Trump.

I have a close friend who is moderately liberal. He is also brilliant, and years ago when I first mentioned the idea to him we would spend hours discussing what this scenario might look like. It was obvious to both of us the conflict would be more about the Establishment vs Outsiders than Democrats vs Republicans. The magnitude of the task confronting such a Suicide President would be immense. I had not yet put a name to the myriad and diverse forces that would be aligned against him, and I didn't yet fully understand how these diverse groups interacted or what the common driving force behind them was, but I was starting to understand that *We the People* were being manipulated by a self-appointed Ruling Class.

I have never been much of a conspiracy advocate. Although I was aware that going all the way back to the days of George H. Bush there were calls among our political elite favoring globalism, I never bought into the theories of a Trilateral Commission conspiracy or any other secret group trying to secretly rule the world.[1] I still don't.

So, my epiphany came when I realized three things…

First, all the disparate factions making up our self-appointed Ruling Class are not held together by formal pacts, secret handshakes, or even by self-identifying with a movement… They are held together by a *culture.* The irony is that they are both its creators and its victims; most of them live in a feedback bubble and are oblivious to the world around them that does not fit their paradigm.[2] Most of them aren't even aware they have created a culture; they believe their worldview is simply what *is*… and that this should be obvious to anyone of any intelligence whatsoever.

My second realization came from my college studies of the philosopher Plato. When I remembered that in his seminal work, The Republic, he advocated for a government that was run by a professional class of ruler, it all started making sense.[3] The Ruling Class culture that has developed in America is largely profession based. Consciously or subconsciously, our self-appointed Ruling Class see themselves as ruling elite… And the culture they have created around themselves gives them feedback permission to do whatever is necessary to exercise that rule. After all, they are 'exactly' what Plato called for – the best and brightest of society – and they have a moral obligation to do what's best for all of us (whether we appreciate it or not).

My third realization was that the unifying force behind all the disparate factions making up our self-appointed Ruling Class *really is* globalism.

So it was with these epiphanies in mind that in early 2015 I said to my friend, "Watch out for Donald Trump."

As were most people at the time, my friend was skeptical that Trump would even run. His name had been tossed around as a candidate in previous elections and while he'd done nothing to dispel the rumors, he'd never actually entered the race. The general consensus was that he simply fueled those rumors to drive publicity for his name and brand. But that's not an impression I ever bought into. When I actually listened to what he was saying (instead of what the media was telling me he was saying) he struck me as a man that was evaluating his opportunities but wisely wasn't in a rush to pull the trigger.

At the time, I knew almost nothing about what kinds of policies Donald Trump would support. Years before I had read his book, *The Art of the Deal*, and knew it to be extremely credible. So, being attracted to the idea that he was not a professional politician, I reread the book. And I read other books. And then came the day when I watched him and Melania descend the escalator at Trump Towers…

Up to this point I had never heard him give a speech. As I watched the live broadcast of his announcement officially declaring himself a candidate for the Presidency, I sat there amazed. He was saying things no other politicians would dare to say.[4] It wasn't hyperbole; it was total truth. He talked about a large number of problems we have here in the United States that never get addressed, including illegal immigration.

In the following days I contemplated that speech. It was very different than any of the other announcement speeches that were occurring left and right. What totally amazed me, however, was the reaction of the media. I actually had to go back and reread the speech several times; I couldn't believe they were talking about the *same* speech I had listened to. They were totally mischaracterizing what I had heard him say. It took a number of conversations with other people I know and respect to understand that different people had heard the same words but some of them had garnered a different meaning. By this time, I had heard him speak a couple more times and I realized something...

I spoke Trump.

Maybe it's because of my life in business and being self-employed, maybe it's because I've had the honor and benefit of working around a number of highly successful business people (or maybe it's just the opposite; maybe it's because I put myself through college tending bar and working third shift in an aircraft plant), but I totally understood what he was saying. I got it. It wasn't the same precise language that politicians use; it was the same no-nonsense straightforward speech I was accustomed to hearing from a certain billionaire, a few foreman, and various other successful empire builders I had known. As a marketing expert I've always understood that people tend to hear what they want to hear, and Trump's way of talking certainly made that easy. Unfortunately for him, at that point in time most people were still assuming he was disingenuous; that his run for office was simply a publicity stunt - and that is what they heard...

I think it is important for readers to understand that at this point StressFreeBill was not promoting *Donald Trump for President*. I was still trying to gauge the field and ascertain the policy positions of all the candidates, including Trump. The problem was, none of the candidates (Republican or Democrat) were really talking about policy... *Except for Donald Trump.*

By then I knew that he was serious about his run even if most others still thought it was a stunt. It was obvious to me that *he* was taking his candidacy seriously. There was zero doubt in my mind he had set being President of the United States as a goal and that he would use the same focused determination to achieve it as he had everything else in his life. I was also getting the feeling that he was exactly the type of outsider that could come in and shake things up, but I still considered him a long shot. I also wanted to know more about what he believed in. Other Republicans were vociferously claiming he wasn't at all conservative – but many of those same Republicans had so bastardized the term that I preferred to reserve judgment. Besides, in a moment of self-realization, it dawned on me that it was more important to put someone in office that would bust up the Washington cartel than it was to have exact ideological alignment...

During the Republican Primary StressFreeBill watched every public speech Donald Trump gave, 99% of them in real time. I personally watched him make fun of a reporter (which was later widely misreported as him making fun of a disability) and I personally watched him verbally strike back against his opponents after they had come hard after him.[5] They didn't have the guts or strength to make the attacks personally, of course; almost all of them had surrogates do the dirty work for them.[6] [7] They then used his directness to paint him as a cretin. The contrast in the type of men (and woman) running against Donald Trump and the streetfighter himself was striking. I watched it all and I came to my conclusion: Donald Trump would be the Republican Nominee for president of the United States.

This was still before the first primary (the Iowa caucus) was held. He lost Iowa, but by now I was all in. I felt strongly that I had found my suicide president. I still didn't know all of his policy positions and there was still a lot of rumor and innuendo that he wasn't a *true* Republican... But I was convinced he was the straight talking street fighting businessman outsider that Washington needed.

An interesting thing happened on the way to the nomination...

By the time Donald Trump was elected the 45th President of the United States on November 8, 2016 he had already accomplished the impossible (in my book). He had forced the fake intellectuals and pseudo-conservatives out of the shadows. Supposedly conservative think tank gurus like Bill Kristol and Eric Erickson had shown their true colors in their vociferous opposition to him.[8] They and their ilk founded the Never Trump movement – even threatening to vote for Hillary Clinton before Trump.[9] And what were their objections? Always some vague ramblings that he wasn't conservative enough, with his insistence on fair trade deals and controlling our borders cited as examples... Well, they were right that he wasn't one of them – but they were not (and still aren't) true conservatives in my book anyway. What they did show, however, was that they supported the globalist concepts of open borders and global redistribution of our wealth through one-sided trade *over and above the welfare of the American people.* Whether these people are deep in the pockets of the multinational corporations or whether they are simply elitists that resent any outsider joining their private club is irrelevant. *Behavior Never Lies* and their behavior continues to brand them. They may call themselves Republicans... They may call themselves conservatives... But they are, in fact, of the Ruling Class Intelligentsia.

In the same way that Trump's candidacy forced our self-appointed Ruling Class Intelligentsia overlords out of hiding, our Ruling Class Politicians (on both sides of the aisle) were being forced to expose themselves as well. On the Democrat side it was the outsider Bernie Sanders as the catalyst. The extreme left ideologues in our country instinctively understood that Hillary Clinton was not one of them... So they rallied around Bernie. And to the astonishment and horror of Democrat leadership, he started winning primaries. In reality, Bernie never stood a chance. The Democrat leadership had long before rigged their primaries to prevent any such outsider from ever gaining power.[10] What was amazing about this election cycle, however, was that their rigging and control of the process was totally exposed. In some ways we should be thankful that the elitist leaders of the Republican Party were simply not as competent as their Democrat counterparts. Republican primaries were not rigged with Superdelegates and, while the Republican elitists stood back in open mouth shock, Donald Trump sailed on to clinch the nomination.

NOTE: This is a good place to make a point about the Democrat party. Their strategy has now backfired on them... Although the Ruling Class Democrats remain firmly in control of the party, all of the enthusiasm is coming from the extreme leftist ideologues on the fringe. The centrist all voted for Trump. The leadership hold over the extremists is tenuous and they are desperately trying to figure out how to get the centrists back without losing the extremists' votes. Currently, they have to keep the extremists satisfied by supporting the RESIST movement; they also have to support it to keep the Ruling Class Oligarchs happy – but it is an election losing strategy and they know it. If this book focuses more on the Republican Party it is simply because of this dynamic – the Ruling Class Democrats are locked into their situation and nothing we (or they) can do in the foreseeable future will alter it.

Anyway, as we said, many Republican Ruling Class Politicians showed their true colors as well. Just like the pseudo-conservatives in the intelligentsia, pseudo-representatives of *We the People* showed they couldn't care less about their campaign promises, party platforms, or even electing a Republican to the presidency. Many of them either joined the Never Trump movement or refused to support Donald Trump in his campaign.[11] *There was such blind hatred for this outsider; they were willing to throw the balance of the Supreme Court leftwards for generations.* Again, the reasons were always vague... Using the same politics of personal destruction that the left specializes in, they constantly denounced his character and motives. They almost never addressed the policies he advocated, and when they did they distorted them terribly. StressFreeBill knows this because *I watched every speech Donald Trump gave...*

Many of these same Ruling Class Politicians continue to obstruct his duly elected agenda to this day.[12] From their behavior it appears that their tactics are to delay as much legislative reform as possible in the hopes that the people will turn on him and he will not win reelection. What they seem not to realize, however, is that this behavior continues to expose them. Senators Lindsey Graham and John McCain, like Majority Leader Mitch McConnell and Speaker of the House Paul Ryan (among others), are now clearly identified as open border globalists and Ruling Class Politicians. They are clearly self-identified by their behavior as having priorities that are at odds with the *Will of the People.*

Since the election, this same 'lifting of the veil' has happened for the Ruling Class Bureaucracy. Political appointees and career bureaucrats alike are being exposed for having their own agenda and prioritizing it over the *Will of the People*, the Rule of Law, and the U.S. Constitution. By not prosecuting obvious felonies and conflicts of interest in the Clinton campaign and Foundation, by perpetuating bogus and slanderous intelligence reports, by appointments of Special Counsel and partisan attorneys to investigate bogus allegations of collusion into already known Russian activities, and by felonious leaking of US intelligence and other privileged information of the White House and government, people like James Clapper, John Brennan, Andrew McCabe, James Comey, their cronies, and others have shown by their behavior that they consider themselves of the Ruling Class and therefore above laws and traditions the rest of us abide by.

From StressFreeBill's perspective, forcing these ruling class denizens out of the shadows may go down as the single biggest accomplishment of the Trump administration.

Author's Note: The purpose of this book is not to convince readers to support any specific policy of Donald Trump. The purpose of this book is to identify America's self-appointed Ruling Class, expose their anti-American agenda, and lay out a working plan to defeat them (a plan that every single reader can participate in). StressFreeBill has come to admire President Trump, but whether you do or not is unimportant – what *is* important is to understand that currently he is the biggest and most effective weapon *We the People* have to fight back against those that would subvert our democracy. This fight will not be decided in the next four or eight years. We will need another Champion, and then another... In the meantime, we need to set the stage for the next several elections. We need to be voting up and down the ticket for true patriots and statesmen – not Ruling Class Politicians. We'll talk more about this in the next to last chapter.

CHAPTER NINETEEN

How It All Fits Together

Once StressFreeBill started identifying the different professional groups making up America's self-appointed Ruling Class, the challenge was to figure out how they all interacted. I will again emphasize that I'm not a big believer in conspiracies so to think that these disparate and sometimes opposing groups had enough of an identity to actually organize, let alone communicate with each other and coordinate, seemed a bit over the top.

This is why my epiphany about the newly created culture was so important. If you are subsumed into a culture that indoctrinates you and daily reinforces the idea that you are smarter than 'the masses,' that you know what's best for everyone, that you are *literally* better equipped to make decisions on behalf of everyone else, and that it is your obligation to guide the rest of us that *just aren't smart enough to understand...* Well, when that's your worldview people will automatically do the things that support their cultural brothers and subvert the things that are detrimental.

Think of it this way... Republicans and Democrats have always been at odds with each other. At the end of the day, however, they were united in the common culture of American Exceptionalism. Today, that is no longer true. They are still at odds, and at the end of the day they are still united, but it is the culture of globalism and elitism that brings them together. Their common culture is the culture of the Ruling Class.

It is worth noting that there are exceptions; not all politicians are Ruling Class Politicians. But it is getting ever harder to find them.

Also note that this sense of elitism is nothing new... The left has claimed moral superiority for decades (if not longer). But the election of President Barack Obama turned this mounting movement into an openly accepted culture. Anti-Americanism no longer had to hide in the shadows and it no longer had to restrict itself to the edges. Mainstream news anchors, pundits, political advisers, civil servants... All were now free to openly proclaim their greater vision – it was no longer out of the mainstream to openly question America's role in the world and our traditional values.

This is an important point to understand. If you were alive in the 1960s, the 'Counterculture' was in the open and unavoidable; it wasn't just a philosophy or ideology. You could *see it* by just turning on the TV or walking down the street; it was in the language, it permeated everything. Whether you were a part of it or not, you knew it was there. Somewhere in the late 1970s this counterculture faded away, but the philosophies and ideology remained among those that would later mentor a new generation of Ruling Class. But it didn't become a true culture again until the election of President Barack Obama.

There is one particular group that gets the overwhelming majority of the credit for rebirthing that culture... The Ruling Class Intelligentsia.

There were actually a number of positive things about that radical 1960s culture; not all of it was anti-American. But there *were* persons among it that bore tremendous resentment and hatred in their hearts. These warped anti-American individuals refused to let that hatred go as everything else faded away around them. These leftists had openly talked about the importance of infiltrating our universities and schools – and they were extremely successful at it. What were once bastions of free-thinking, free-speech, and diversity of thought were ill-prepared to resist a conscious takeover by what was then a very small but determined radical group of people that detested traditional American values. As we look back we can see that it was literally like a cancer; step-by-step through professorships, then tenure, then administrative positions... an anti-American philosophy started spreading exponentially. Children of the very wealthy have always been especially vulnerable to anarchist and rebellious thought, and the students of our Ivy League schools proved to be no exception. Unlike today, where the leftist teachings permeate every aspect of college life, these philosophies were originally restricted to certain fields of study. Liberal arts colleges started churning out generation after generation of students educated to *see a higher truth* beyond American Exceptionalism. These students went on to become journalists, politicians, diplomats, attorneys and law clerks. Many worked as civil servants and spread their cynicism about America throughout the government, especially in the State Department. They would eventually permeate every Federal Department including GSA, EPA, IRS, Education, and even the Intelligence Services. The culture in most Federal Departments is now such that a conservative keeps his or her politics to themselves lest they damage their career opportunities.

Some of the attorneys indoctrinated through these philosophies eventually became judges. Some of the civil servants rose to the highest positions of civil service – Assistant Directorships and other positions of power just below the political appointees.

The same happened in the field of journalism. Those former students are now editors, directors, and producers for newspapers and networks and cable news shows. Like attracts like, and personnel in those organizations are now so polarized that 96% of their personal political donations for the 2016 Presidential campaign went to the Ruling Class Democrat candidate, Hillary Clinton.[1]

Politics has always been a dirty business, and historically when newly elected representatives march off to Washington they are quickly faced with the harsh reality of *Go Along or Get Crushed*. Each party has always had its quotas for how much fundraising each member is responsible for, and if you don't meet it, you don't get committee assignments.[2] The lobbyists representing Corporate America have always understood this and have always been ready to help. Resist or complain and you won't get funding for your re-election campaign. Go public and you'll discover that your private donors are now supporting your Primary opponent and your after office private-sector career opportunities have dried up. A fledgling politician soon discovers that he or she is just a cog in the party machine – play along and have a long and lucrative career, or go rogue and go home. This was the political reality even before the anti-American elitist culture of our current Ruling Class set in. But that cynicism is what paved the way for today's abject abandonment of American values and tradition. For these Ruling Class Politicians, privately agreeing that America's role in the world should by necessity be reduced and her wealth redistributed was only a small step further down the road to total self-interest and political survival. Or, maybe they've just always cared more about their own careers than they do our country? It is a distinction without meaning.

It is important to distinguish between leftist and globalists.

The financial impetus behind the globalist movement appears to be more economic than ideological. Ruling Class Oligarchs view globalism as much more beneficial to their business interests and therefore do everything in their power to bring that about. Leftist ideology is simply a convenient way to get there.

The globalist Ruling Class Oligarchy uses the leftist movement and its inherent socialism simply as a tool to bring about their world vision. What is of convenience is that the leadership of the Democrat party long ago sold out the traditional American values of capitalism, self-reliance, and hard work as keys to success. Thirty years ago, and after two terms of President Reagan, no one faction could supply the votes needed to effectively oppose the Republicans. They desperately needed to form coalitions in order to amass enough votes to defeat Republican candidates. No one faction could supply them, so they invited everyone...

"Do you believe trees are more important than people? Then come join us," the Democrats said. *"We'll give you a home and a voice. Do you believe in communism and socialism? No problem! Welcome to our party! You don't believe in God? Well, if you can bring a bunch of votes with you we'll defend your right to be offended by others that do! Don't like living in a masculine world? Come join us and we'll do everything we can to punish men! Are you gay, black, or any other kind of minority? Well, the Republicans are your oppressors so vote for us and we'll give you special status and protections against them..."*

Although it took a number of years, it was relatively easy for the Democrat party to meld a number of different factions that originally had little in common into a united anti-American driving force. A driving force that was easily appropriated by the globalists.

The Republican takeover was much more subtle. Traditional American values had been the bedrock of this party for far longer; the globalists now rising to leadership positions within the party had to tread carefully... they didn't dare openly embrace the core concepts of globalism (such as redistribution of national wealth and reduced American sovereignty). Instead, they talked about Free Trade.

We have discussed how the left is so much better at branding; this is a perfect example. Republican globalists borrowed the leftist tactic of subverting the language. Free Trade has never meant that America should let itself be taken to the cleaners; it has never meant we needed to drop all protections against currency manipulation and other abusive, unfair, and unbalanced trade tactics. Yet the Ruling Class Republicans - just like they were quick to claim the mantle of *conservative* - were now justifying America's dramatic trade imbalances and the rape of the American Middle Class as *Free Trade*. What is amazing and telling are the reactions of the media, other politicians, and pundits... *No one called them out on this!*

As we previously mentioned, the election of President Barack Obama emboldened all these Ruling Class forces. They were convinced that their hold on power was consolidated and that their march towards their *better future* was unstoppable. The Transpacific Partnership (TPP) treaty was almost ready to be ratified, the Obama administration had all but decimated our abilities to defend our borders on both a federal and state level. Our population was swelling at record rates with refugees and emigrants (both legal and illegal) who were resistant to assimilation, and the ranks of the welfare class and others that were dependent upon the handouts of the federal government had swollen to all-time highs. America's leadership on the world stage was in full retreat, and the historically unifying force of Christianity that had given America its fundamental values was now seemingly a persecuted minority. Domestically, the radical forces of the left controlled the streets; and internationally, disruptive forces of terrorism caused never-ending fear – and the violence of both went unopposed. The media was in full control of the agenda.

It is no wonder, then, that the Ruling Class was arrogant and confident. Perfect evidence of this would be the Gang of Eight Comprehensive Immigration Reform package that Republicans and Democrats tried so hard to pass. Amnesty and the giving of welfare and other social and educational benefits to illegal aliens was extremely unpopular amongst the Republican base. Yet, here were four Republican senators (along with four Democrat senators) openly and publicly pushing for just that. The four Democrat senators were Michael Bennett (D–CO), Richard Durbin (D–IL), Robert Menendez (D–NJ), and Charles Schumer (D–NY). The four Republican senators were Jeff Flake (R–AZ), Lindsey Graham (R–SC), John McCain (R–AZ), and Marco Rubio (R–FL).

Do those last four Republican names sound familiar? They should… They were *Never Trumpers* and/or vociferously opposed the election of Donald Trump… and to this day they obstruct, criticize, undermine, and do everything within their power to paint public opinion against him.

So, is President Donald Trump the perfect anti-Ruling Class superhero?

Honestly? It's too early to tell. StressFreeBill was thrilled when late in the presidential campaign Donald Trump started talking about *Draining the Swamp*. It was a validation that I had read the man correctly; he wanted to be President to get things done and he was willing to declare political war to make it happen. This is exactly what I had been calling for all those years ago in my discussions about a suicide President. He was a fighter that talked about standing up to the Ruling Class. During the campaign I was constantly pleased and surprised that Donald Trump's positions seemed more and more to parallel conservative thought. I was, however, under no illusions that he was an ideological conservative; it was apparent to me that Donald Trump is not an ideologue. I can only fall back on my explanation that StressFreeBill *speaks Trump*... But it was obvious to me that he was searching for the most logical, efficient, and practical ways to get things done. Since conservatism is pretty much based on the same thing, many of our views were in parallel, but I was fully prepared for differences.

The current GOP proposed healthcare replacement is a good example of this. As this book is being written, the Ruling Class politicians in the Republican Party are trying to stall the repeal of Obamacare, but barring that jam a different big government healthcare package down our throats. StressFreeBill is fully convinced that what the American people have been clamoring for is anything but this... We have wanted repeal of Obamacare, *not replacement*. In other words, get the government out of it altogether – even remove the monopoly creating restrictions of state lines, etc. Require transparency in pricing and let the free market and natural competition lower the cost of healthcare itself and, therefore, the insurance that helps people afford it. The government can backstop the industry by subsidizing High-risk Pools, but that should be its only direct involvement.

Donald Trump sees healthcare as a legitimate responsibility of government; conservatives do not. It is simply an ideological difference. To draw a line here and stop supporting our President because of this one issue would be to win the battle yet lose the war. Healthcare is an ideological difference I am willing to accept *if* he is a leader that can bust the Ruling Class Culture. And make no mistake, nothing short of culture busting will save America. This is a war – a culture war. For clarity, StressFreeBill is not advocating violence in any form… But the dangers to life, liberty, and the pursuit of happiness are just as real today as they were in 1776. Perhaps even more so, because the oppressive forces aligned against us are just as strong but much more subtle.

As of now, President Donald Trump is our Champion. Just as armies and tribes of old would choose champions to fight in single combat to decide issues, he is the man we have chosen to wield his sword against the evil forces of the Ruling Class. The battle has just begun and we cannot know yet whether he is a superhero… After all, superheroes always win.

The war is just beginning…

The election of Donald Trump sent shockwaves throughout the Ruling Class. Some of the best evidence that StressFreeBill is correct when talking about a Ruling Class culture in America is the reaction that rippled through entire professions. The immediate reaction of the Ruling Class was a well-funded effort to refute the election and undermine the democratic process. Ruling Class Intelligentsia called for members of the Electoral College to abandon the will of the people and place their vote for Hillary Clinton regardless of how the people voted. The Ruling Class Media promoted and supported this idea. The Ruling Class Oligarchy financed it and Ruling Class Politicians on both sides of the aisle *didn't condemn it*.

When that effort failed, Ruling Class Politicians committed to slow walking Trump administration appointments to cabinet, departmental, and judicial positions.[3] [4] By their actions and inactions politicians on both sides of the aisle, and especially the Senate leadership, are guilty of this. This, in effect, has left a large amount of the Obama administration in place within the Executive Branch. For a large number of reasons this has been critical for the Ruling Class and their battle to maintain control.

The Obama White House had politicized every department in government. The scandalous results are too numerous to list in their entirety, but they include the ATF selling guns to Mexican cartels in a failed effort to create public outcry for gun control, the IRS targeting Tea Party groups and other conservative voices, the State Department looking the other way as Hillary Clinton used the Clinton foundation in a pay-for-play scheme, the BLM confiscating large swaths of private property and declaring them off limits to energy production and development, and the Justice Department all but federalizing certain metropolitan police forces in order to allow and promote racial disharmony.[5] [6] [7] [8] [9] [10] Especially nefarious was the politicization and weaponization of the historically impartial FBI and our intelligence services.[11] [12]

James Comey, who at the time was the director of the FBI, had presided over some of the most egregiously biased non-investigations in the history of the agency. Credible books were being published and movies were being made detailing the corruption of the Clinton Foundation, it's collusion with foreign governments, and our own State Department. At least one of the books was heavily researched and complete with references, citations, and stated sources.[7] Yet, the FBI declined to investigate this alleged corruption permeating the highest levels of our government.

Meanwhile, the Obama administration was in the process of once again violating *The People's trust*. After 9/11, President George W. Bush signed the Patriot Act. This legislation gave previously unheard of powers to our intelligence agencies to monitor our private lives. It was argued that this loss of rights was minimal and necessary to protect against the terrorism dangers of the modern world. Whether that argument is valid or not, it was accompanied by unwavering promises and guarantees that it would not be a slippery slope – that the government would not be on a continual pursuit to expand their surveillance powers and violate the privacy of citizens. The promises and guarantees proved to be a sham. The Obama administration used and abused these powers by directing the NSA (and others) to spy on their political enemies.[13] FISA court protocols were ignored and surveillance warrants were issued illegally.[14] The boldness of this reckless ignoring of law and Constitutional protections is a testament to the absolute control they felt they had over the American people. None of these illegalities would be allowed the light of day under the upcoming eight-year presidential reign of Hillary Clinton, so they felt completely safe. Oops.

The Clinton campaign was so shaken they immediately looked for excuses; starting the very night of her loss they began formulating a strategy to blame it on Russian interference.[30]

If it was embarrassing for Hillary, this cataclysmic miscalculation caused a sense of desperation amongst the Ruling Class Bureaucracy of the intelligence communities. In order to protect themselves, the Trump presidency had to be undermined, thwarted, and removed by forced resignation or impeachment. It was bad enough that the new President was an outsider, but now people's careers and even potential indictments were at stake. Other factions of our Ruling Class were only too happy to aid in the effort. At first blush this would seem a tall order, but StressFreeBill reminds the reader of the arrogance of the Ruling Class – and after all, it's not like our intelligence services have never caused foreign governments to fall, right?

Although it is still unclear who the specific instigator was, the intelligence services were complicit in the *creation of a bogus dossier* centered around the alleged actions of Donald Trump and the Russian government.[20] [21] This dossier included bogus allegations of Trump hiring prostitutes in a Russian hotel and of meetings of his campaign staff with Russian officials. In the meantime, scrambling to avert their own public exposure and not wanting a public record of what could be damaging information, the Democratic National Committee (DNC) *refused* to allow our intelligence services access to their computer server that had allegedly been hacked.[23] Instead, they hired a private firm, CrowdStrike, to do the investigation and provide a forensic analysis. The fact that CrowdStrike has close ties to the Democrat party was totally ignored by Ruling Class Politicians on both sides of the aisle as well as the Ruling Class Media.[24] [25] Based *only* on this *partisan third-party analysis*, Ruling Class Bureaucrats in our intelligence services announced that the Russians had hacked into our elections. The Ruling Class Media quickly and incorrectly reported that all 17 US intelligence agencies had signed off on this conclusion. In fact, it was only four agencies (of which only three expressed 'high confidence'), and it has been reported that only a single person from each agency was responsible for the evaluation.[26] [27] So, it appears that four Ruling Class bureaucrats issued a finding (based on a server they never inspected) that the Russians hacked our elections. Using a joke that Trump publically made, *'Maybe the Russians can find Hillary's missing 30,000 emails,'* they conflated the server finding, the bogus dossier, and the joke into the accusation that the Trump campaign colluded with the Russians. This easily plugged into the excuse of this being the only reason Hillary lost the election.[20] [22] [28] [29]

One can only assume that their desperation was high and the time was short; little else could explain such a flimsy frame-up being put in place. Yet, the Ruling Class Media (without any investigative journalism) went on a nonstop months-long tirade accusing the Trump campaign of colluding with the Russian government to influence the outcome of the Presidential election.

Undaunted, the Trump administration consistently refuted the allegations and continued with its pursuit of draining the swamp. This included the firing of FBI director James Comey, which still left the agency in the charge of now Acting Director of the FBI, Andrew McCabe (who has ties to top Clinton donors and allies).[15] So, while the Ruling Class still had their man in charge at the FBI, this brought them one-step closer to losing control of that agency.

Meanwhile, Ruling Class Politicians and Media had successfully pressured Attorney General Sessions to recuse himself from the investigation. This provided the Ruling Class with the opening they needed and left the Justice Department under the control of the Deputy Attorney General Rod Rosenstein. He proceeded to appoint Robert Mueller (a good friend of James Comey) as Special Counsel to investigate the allegations of Russian interference in US elections. One of the first acts of Robert Mueller was to hire a number of partisan investigators which included Democrat donors and even one attorney who represented the Clinton Foundation. Thus, the Ruling Class now has a hammer in place that can spend the next four years pounding away at President Trump and everyone in his administration (including his family). They can and will expand the investigation well beyond the scope of Russia and will publically and mercilessly prosecute to the fullest extent of the law even the smallest of technical infractions they will inevitably discover. This represents a very serious threat to the *Will of the People*... With business holdings as large as the Trump's it will be easy to find various technical violations here or there. With the Ruling Class Media to help them, the Special Counsel will do their best to inflate and prosecute even the most insignificant of infractions. They will not stop until people go to jail. They will not stop until the President resigns.

So, to summarize...

The Ruling Class Politicians and Bureaucrats of the Obama administration got caught with their pants down when Hillary Clinton lost the election. They were spying on the American people and were in imminent danger of being exposed. In addition, the illegal activities of DNC members as well as Hillary Clinton while she served as Secretary of State, along with the alleged money laundering activities of the Clinton Foundation would not bear close scrutiny.[7] [16] With multiple motivations (not the least of which was CYA) the Resistance movement was formed. With Ruling Class Oligarchs like George Soros funding highly visible protests and marches, and Ruling Class Politicians slow walking the replacement of Obama appointees and allies, and while Ruling Class Bureaucrats created and leaked a false narrative of Russian collusion, the entire Ruling Class culture dedicated itself to subversion.[17] [3] [18] The Ruling Class Media did its part to fan the flames on a daily basis and overhyped a narrative *they knew to be false.*[19] The Ruling Class Bureaucracy also managed to appoint a

Special Counsel to further undermine the Trump administration by holding a highly publicized and supposedly independent investigation into claims that were *already known to be false*. The investigation, coincidentally, is being conducted by the Ruling Class Bureaucracy itself and certainly has the goal of persecuting and prosecuting members of the Trump Administration.

StressFreeBill, under a different pen name, is a best-selling science fiction author – and even I couldn't make this stuff up.

It would be easy, on the one hand, to despair at the sheer magnitude of forces assembled against *We the People*. We must be very careful, however, not to let the trees in front of us block us from seeing the forest...

While the onslaught of accusations, falsehoods, and character assassination being thrown at the Trump administration is unprecedented, StressFreeBill sees them as acts of desperation.

The Ruling Class has been knocked back on its heels.

I cannot think of a single professional politician that could have stood up to what Donald Trump has had to face – yet he still stands. He bypasses the Ruling Class Media and goes direct to the people with social media. He fights back. He calls out reporters and networks for lying and publishing fake news. He's not afraid to publicly ask about the questionable activities of the previous administration. He daily sends the Ruling Class Media on wild goose chases with morning tweets designed to infuriate and distract them, and then quietly goes about doing the business of *the People* and fulfilling his campaign promises. He takes care of veterans; he puts people back to work...

StressFreeBill has to admit that he's been very impressed by Donald J Trump. And there is more reason for optimism about America's future now than there has been in over 20 years... But the battles have barely started and it will take every single one of us to achieve victory.

StressFreeBill is writing this book because he loves America and wants to do his part in protecting her, but no one person can win the war. President Donald Trump cannot defeat America's self-appointed Ruling Class by himself. I certainly can't accomplish anything by myself. We need you, the American people. Every single one of us. The next chapter will discuss what we as individuals can do to take our country, and *our culture*, back.

CHAPTER TWENTY

How to Make a Difference

Many years ago someone told me that politically I mattered, that I could make a difference in the world around me. I half smiled in response and gave a polite nod. It took a long time for me to understand that he was right. He wasn't right because of any special skills I harbor; he was right because I am a free individual with a voice and a vote.

Being politically active doesn't mean attending a bunch of rallies or knocking on doors or volunteering your time... Being politically active simply means paying a little bit of attention and contributing your part – *even if it's just with the language you use...*

If you've made it this far through the book I'm assuming you more or less agree with me on most points. Or, at least agree with me that there is a Ruling Class culture that is taking America in the wrong direction. If not, well... I've given it my best try and I'll just ask you to keep an open mind as you continue observing this crazy political world we live in.

But, for the moment, let's assume we agree with each other enough to think that something must be done... What can we do?

StressFreeBill has put years of thought into that answer. Many of the suggestions you read here have been borrowed from other great minds. My goal is to take all of these great solutions and put them together into an effective and easy to implement strategy *every single one of us can participate in.*

This strategy will be divided up into several short suggestions. Each solution is simple and in many cases require very little, if any, of your time. What they do require is a willingness on your part to make a difference and a dedication to seeing it through.

And lastly, before we discuss the solutions, let's make sure we have absolute clarity on what the goal is. StressFreeBill sums it up like this:

> My goal is to expose, reject, undermine, and render impotent the anti-American Ruling Class culture that is attempting to take control of our country. I will do this by working within the law in a nonviolent manner. I understand that changing or replacing a culture is a long-term effort based upon winning the hearts and minds of people rather than trying to control what they can say and do. I will use my influence and my voice to support other champions of American ideals, and I will have the strength to speak truth to the powerful elite that stand against them. I will be ever confident that my voice, added with millions of others, will carry the day and ensure that *"Government of the people, by the people, and for the people shall not perish from earth."*

Suggestion #1: Politics is downstream from culture, but culture is downstream from language. If you want to change a culture, then change your language.

We've already mentioned how the left, and now the Ruling Class, have traditionally been much better at using language than we have. Terms like conservative, alt-right, pro-choice, climate denier, free trade, and progressive are all misappropriated terms and labels purposely used to shape public opinion or mask true intentions. If you understand branding, however, it can also be used to unmask absurdity and duplicity.

Our mainstream media provides an outstanding opportunity for us to turn the tables. According to a 2016 Pew Research study, *only 18%* of Americans have high trust in national news outlets.[1] Even when you add in local media (which carry a much higher level of trust) only 32% have a great deal or fair amount of trust in the media.[2] Everyone knows that the media is biased. Everyone knows that the news is slanted. The only people that pretend differently are journalists themselves. It's time to shout, *'The Emperor has no clothes.'*

StressFreeBill no longer refers to the national media as mainstream or liberal or even biased... I simply refer to them as the Ruling Class Media. I don't do it with any special animus; I don't put any special emphasis on the words when I speak... I have simply incorporated the title Ruling Class into my everyday language. I actually do the same thing when I'm talking about certain politicians and other factions, but the *Ruling Class Media meme* has the greatest potential to shape public perception.

Most Americans when hearing the term *Ruling Class* immediately understand that it identifies people that believe themselves superior, have different priorities, and exercise power and control. It implies that everyone not in the Ruling Class group are commoners; that they are the rulers and we are the ruled. Because this is in actuality how the Ruling Class Media behaves, it carries the imprimatur of truth. The American people are fed up with the media and fed up with being manipulated; branding them as Ruling Class provides an outlet for all of this built up angst. Exposing your would-be oppressors feels good.

For those politicians who meet the definition of Ruling Class (of which there are many), such a label can be devastating. Public faith in senators and congressmen polls not much higher than the media. This lack of faith and trust by the American people is well deserved. When discussing certain political activities with others, StressFreeBill does not hesitate to label a deserving politician as a *Ruling Class Politician*. This usually leads to an opening to simply explain that the politician in question has their own agenda, is mostly concerned about donors and reelection, and obviously doesn't care about the Will of the People. StressFreeBill has yet to meet anyone that doesn't immediately comprehend the appropriateness of the term. Even my friends and acquaintances that are submerged in the political world and resent the label cannot argue it's brazenness of truth.

StressFreeBill is asking all of us to exercise the casual influence we each carry in our everyday interactions. I encourage you to start using this label in *all* of your social media postings and casual conversations about politics. If you have the ability to contact *influencers* in our society, people with a public voice, please do so. StressFreeBill is on a mission to make the terms *Ruling Class Media* and *Ruling Class Politician* part of the American lexicon. This is a tall order and will not happen overnight, but it is the single most-powerful weapon we could employ against the ruling class culture. It might seem counterintuitive to think that something so simple could have such a large effect, but as a marketing expert I can promise you it is real. If these terms become a common part of the everyday American political lexicon, it will spell the beginning of the end for the ruling class culture. As Rush Limbaugh would say, *"Don't doubt me on this!"*

If you need help explaining this concept to someone you have my permission (with accreditation) to copy, reprint, and distribute these few paragraphs under **Suggestion #1**. Or, you could give them a copy of this book. What is probably easiest, however, is to go to the www.StressFreeBill.com website and under *Simple Truths* you can select the article, *Why Call Them the Ruling Class Media?* You can tweet and/or share the article on Facebook and other social media (or send it as a private message). You can also register to receive StressFreeBill's blog posts as email - this will keep you up-to-date on Ruling Class interference in current events.

Suggestion #2: Take entertainment from the Ruling Class Media, but take your news from carefully vetted sources.

Stop trusting the Ruling Class Media. It's as simple as that. Well, it *is* simple to say it... But it's not easy to do. If you follow politics it's not at all easy to escape the sensationalism we are all bombarded with daily. It doesn't make any difference what your network of choice is; they all fight for ratings and clamor for your attention. When you do watch, it is very important to remember that they are trying to influence you. *Remember, the Ruling Class Media has a vested interest in trying to make you feel like a lonely isolated voice swimming against the tide of inevitability.* They want you to feel as if your views represent only an insignificant minority – *it simply isn't true.* On the StressFreeBill.com website we discuss the difference between leadership and manipulation, but the Ruling Class Media is *absolutely* trying to manipulate you. On that same website I provide a list of media figures that I believe prioritize truth. I also include a partial list of some of the most egregious manipulators in the Ruling Class Media. These are *my* opinions based on *my* observations, and if they help you I'm happy to provide them... *but you should make your own evaluations.*

You can pick *any* network and in any given news hour observe anchors, hosts, and pundits attempt to question, explain, or act bewildered at the actions of Congress, the bureaucracy, or President Trump. How many times do we need to watch a Fox News host lament, *"Why can't the Republicans get their act together and pass healthcare (or, whatever)... What is going on?"* It is frustrating to watch people with such a public platform cover current events in a way that *you know* to be misleading, incomplete, and/or a flat out lie.

There is nothing bewildering about what is going on if you understand it is about the Ruling Class vs *We the People*, not Democrats vs Republicans.

Most people perceive the national media as divided by bias to the left and bias to the right... I would argue that these definitions are no longer accurate. I will agree that the *liberal* media has totally sold out to the Ruling Class, *but much of the so-called conservative media have as well...*

Even Fox News and Fox Business News (FBN) showcase a large number of Ruling Class Media hosts, anchors, and pundits. While some of them may be disingenuous, others are probably just too young or inexperienced to perceive the Ruling Class cultural bubble they are immersed in - *but that doesn't make any difference.* It is behavior we are concerned with; not motivation. You must not trust these people or allow them to influence your emotions and attitudes about current events and the direction of the country.

It is also my belief that CNN, MSNBC, NBC news, the Associated Press (AP), the New York Times, and the Washington Post (among others) are news outlets that have lost all journalistic credibility and have simply become propaganda outlets to manipulate people to their worldview.

Before believing anything you hear from the media, StressFreeBill strongly suggests that you get into the habit of checking the source and byline (network and/or reporter). We should not risk being misinformed by believing in non-credible sources – and it's time we admit publicly and to ourselves who is and is not any longer credible.

A tactic I personally use is to, as much as possible, listen directly to the source of information instead of letting the media interpret or condense what was said. In other words, I listen directly to President Trump's speeches, rallies, and press conferences. I do the same for Paul Ryan, Mitch McConnell, Nancy Pelosi, Chuck Schumer, and Adam Schiff. I watch the White House press conferences (as opposed to the soundbites shared on network news). I get my information from *the horse's mouth* rather than trusting the media not to color it.

I realize that many people do not have the same amount of time as StressFreeBill does to devote to these activities. Therefore, my best suggestion is to carefully decide who in the national media you can trust *not to alter facts*. In my opinion, it is okay if they are partisan – I just want to make sure they are not going to alter the information to push an agenda.

At the request of one of my proofreaders for this book I will include a few names that I trust *not to alter information* (which doesn't mean I always agree with their conclusions). Please be aware that this is a very incomplete list…

StressFreeBill's sources of information include, but are not limited to: Lou Dobbs (FBN), Charles Hurt (Washington Times), Tammy Bruce (Fox News), Newt Gingrich (former Speaker of the House), Mike Huckabee (former governor of Arkansas), Catherine Herridge (Fox News), James Delingpole (English columnist and novelist), Sean Hannity (Fox News),

Tucker Carlson (Fox News), Rush Limbaugh (radio host), James O'Keefe (Project Veritas), Sara Carter (Circa News), John Solomon (Circa News), Judge Jeanine Pirro (Fox News), Peter Schweizer (investigative journalist and novelist), and Jay Sekulow (Chief Counsel for the American Center for Law and Justice).

For those that are interested in my take on current events, you can register to follow my blog at www.StressFreeBill.com.

Suggestion #3: Treat Primaries with the same seriousness you give General Elections.

For a lot of reasons the 2016 GOP Presidential Primary race attracted more attention than any primary in memory. If you are like most people, however, you typically don't pay a lot of attention to the primaries... especially in an off-Presidential election year. It's understandable; people have things to do and lives to lead... and the candidates all tend to sound the same, speak the same, and promise the same things (which they will many times go on to ignore after being elected).

This is, however, one of the weaknesses in our two-party system that the Ruling Class has learned to exploit. By the time the general election rolls around to elect a President, Senator, or Congressman, the non-Ruling Class Politicians have many times been already eliminated. Democrats and Republicans will always be in different camps, but at the end of the day if all the candidates for an office are of the Ruling Class what difference does our general election vote really make?

The Ruling Class wins either way and *We the People* lose. Again.

One thing we must remember about the Ruling Class... They don't just believe they have better *ideas* on how to run the government, they believe they are the only ones *at all competent* to run our government. They don't see Ruling Class candidates being the only option for voters as undemocratic; they arrogantly see it as necessary and even patriotic.

Think of it like this... An MD might recommend surgery to alleviate back pain whereas a chiropractor might recommend spinal decompression therapy. Both highly respectable doctors might strongly argue for their solution as the best treatment plan, but at the end of the day they would both recognize each other as competent health professionals. What if, instead, the patient decided to trust the diagnosis and treatment recommended by his plumber? This is so obviously absurd, and the medical profession protects its integrity so strongly that it has been made illegal; you cannot practice medicine without a license.

Professional politicians look at things the same way. The thought of any outsider(s) running the government is just as absurd. Republicans and Democrats might diagnose problems differently and suggest opposing solutions, but at the end of the day they recognize each other as professionals and, therefore, the only ones competent to run the government. The problem is, our political system was never set up to be run by a professional class – and there are certainly no laws against practicing politics without a license. The Constitution of the United States does not provide for a professional political class and the Bill of Rights specifically gives *We the People* protections against it.

Being an elected official was never meant to be a profession (or a career). The fallacy of the arrogant Ruling Class culture is that they believe themselves to have special skills and arcane knowledge unavailable to other professions. StressFreeBill has no doubt that they would strenuously deny this attitude, but we are engaged in observing behavior *and they behave exactly as if theirs is a protected profession that can only be entered by an extensive peer-reviewed vetting process.*

Not to belabor the point, but this is in direct opposition to the Constitution of the United States which gives us a political system that can only be entered by an extensive *We the People reviewed election process.*

So, the Ruling Class has learned to stack the deck in the primaries where few people are paying attention. Most people registered as Democrat or Republican more or less tend to trust their parties; they pop their heads up around election time, get a feel (as much as they can) for what the issues are, vote for their party's recommended candidate, and then go back to living their lives. This, again, is especially true for Senate and Congressional elections that fall directly between Presidential elections.

The Democrat primaries, as we discussed previously, are in many ways rigged to a much larger extent than the Republican's... And while what we are discussing applies to them as well, for a number of reasons I will focus mainly on GOP primary candidates...

The Ruling Class exploitation of our GOP primaries is another huge point StressFreeBill is making in his argument to start labeling Ruling Class Politicians for what they are. People need a reason to vote in the primaries. Simply arguing that one candidate is better, or more true, or more conservative than another candidate has proven insufficient to gain the attention and interest of the vast majority of registered Republicans. This is one reason that incumbents win reelection over 90% of the time. While it has been easy for politicians to appropriate the label *conservative*, StressFreeBill thinks it would be much harder for a politician to run away from the label *Ruling Class* – unless they have the behavior (voting record) to show differently. This means, if we can change the conversation and give the people a distinction they can readily grasp, we will have a more engaged voter base. When the foremost focus of a primary election is on which politician actually follows the mandate of the voters (rather than arrogantly trying to rule us by following their own agenda) voters *do* step up to the plate...

A good example of this was the 2017 GOP gubernatorial primary in Virginia. Ed Gillespie, a long-time well-known member of the GOP Ruling Class, ran against Corey Stewart and Frank Wagner for the nomination. The conventional wisdom was that Virginia, with its tens of thousands of government employees, would be firmly in the camp of the big government Ruling Class – therefore Gillespie was expected to win easily. He staffed his campaign almost exclusively with establishment Never Trumpers and took pains on the campaign trail to distance himself from the President. His main opponent, on the other hand, embraced President Trump and his *America First* philosophy. The results of this primary election have sent shockwaves throughout the entire Ruling Class establishment. The underfunded and pro-Trump Corey Stewart, whose previously highest held office had been a County Board of Supervisors, came within just over a point of defeating Gillespie. What's more, if you add in Frank Wagner's votes, the pro-Trump anti-Ruling Class votes would have overwhelmed Ed Gillespie in a landslide.[3] [4]

The Ruling Class is immersed in a culture that is incapable of believing that *We the People* can't plainly see that they are best suited to rule us. Close elections like this may stun them, but they still fully expect the people to come to their senses and eventually walk away from President Trump. They are incapable of seeing through their bubble to understand that *they* are what the people have rejected. As shocked as they are by how close this primary election was, it will not shatter their worldview. They will continue their duplicitous 'nonsupport', obstruction, and outright subversion of the *Will of the People* as expressed through the election of Donald Trump.

We must replace them. We must remove them from office. It is fallacy to hope that they will 'come around', 'wake up', and 'smell the roses...'

Gillespie's opponents tried to brand him as a *Washington Insider*, but StressFreeBill is not convinced that the connotations of that label are clearly negative to the average GOP voter, and after all, he's still a Republican (so how bad can he be). One cannot help but wonder, however, how much success they might've had if they would have given the voters a much clearer distinction. What if they would have branded him as a Ruling Class Politician? In a primary election that was decided by less than 5,000 votes, it might have made all the difference.

We have discussed at length in this book how both Democrat and GOP Ruling Class Politicians are opposing, stalling, and subverting the agenda of President Donald Trump. They will continue to believe that the people will eventually reject him up until the day his second term in office expires… However, they will simply view that day as the beginning of a return to *business as normal* – this is why they are doing everything possible to stall his reform efforts until that day arrives. They will not acknowledge a new direction in America; they will not admit to being defeated by 'populism'. If *We the People* truly desire for President Trump to drain the swamp, and if we want those gains to last longer than eight years, then we must help him now. We must immediately start replacing the Ruling Class Politicians in Washington DC. StressFreeBill totally rejects the idea that you must be a professional politician to serve as an elected official. I couldn't care less whether we replace them with plumbers, attorneys, factory workers, insurance salesman, doctors, or stay at home mothers… As long as they are intelligent individuals that can be transparent with the American people, have a keen interest in the issues facing us, and as long as they are true patriots that will place America First,

StressFreeBill will vote for them. And I hope you will too.

I have set up a website dedicated to this purpose, www.PrimaryTheRulingClass.com. Every two years there is a Senate, Congressional, and/or Presidential election. The six-months-to-a-year preceding these elections are when the primaries are held. Depending upon when you read this book, it may be before, during, or after a primary election. Regardless of the timing, I recommend that you go to this site and bookmark it now. As each election approaches we will highlight the GOP primary candidates and help our readers identify (by compiling behavioral evidence) which incumbents and challengers are Ruling Class Politicians and which are not. It is my hope that you will support the anti-Ruling Class candidates *even if you do not live in their representative districts or states*.

This is a nationwide movement to save our representative style of government, and StressFreeBill invites you to join it.

Suggestion #4: Use your voice; make others aware of the self-appointed Ruling Class.

Some people avoid talking about politics as much as possible. Others obsess about it and will turn every conversation into a political debate. If you're reading this book I'm guessing you're somewhere in the middle.

To be effective in exposing the self-appointed Ruling Class you don't have to ambush and chase away your friends or become obsessive, but you do need to say *something*...

You can do it in casual conversation or by purposely bringing up the subject, but declaring your belief and/or frustration and *putting a name to it* is important. We're playing the long game here, so it's not necessary to do this in every single conversation you have with everyone you know or meet... But you do need to get into the habit of using the terms *Ruling Class*, *Ruling Class Politician*, and *Ruling Class Media*. If you find someone curious or receptive don't hesitate to use *third-party credibility* to make your case. Refer them to this book or the StressFreeBill.com website. Then, be sure to follow up the next time you speak with them by simply asking what they thought of the book/website. Most will probably not have looked at it, and that's okay. But *asking* if they've seen the information is important. Expert marketers will tell you about the incredible influencing power of this second, or even a third, follow-up. This isn't being pushy; it is simply being honestly curious and asking, "What did you like best about the book (or website)?"

If you are a little bit more ambitious, consider calling into a radio station and talking about the Ruling Class Media. Letters to the editor or leaving comments on a news site's webpage can also be influential. Social media is a powerful way to spread influencing memes... And even a little bit of strategic coordination is a force multiplier. Feel free to *share* various articles about the Ruling Class from the StressFreeBill.com website to your friends and followers on Facebook, Twitter, Instagram, Google+, etc. Post the articles on your social media sites and add a comment that includes the words *Ruling Class* – the more often these words are used the faster they become part of the lexicon.

You don't have to print T-shirts or coffee mugs to get the message out (even though I'm doing that very thing on StressFreeBill.com)... Simply have the confidence of your convictions and care about the future of our country. Other people will see and respect this.

It will feel good to do your part – even if it is only a seemingly small thing. There's a lot to be said for knowing you contributed to a common cause. If you have children it's probably a good example to set; if you have parents it's probably something that would make them proud. Doing something – big or small – is better than standing on the sidelines... And no matter what else happens in life, you'll always be glad you did.

Suggestion #5: Donate your money; every $10 counts.

In his 2016 presidential campaign, Donald Trump raised over $239 million from small donations ($200 or less). This set a new record; it was more in small donations than Obama raised in 2012 and it was more than Hillary Clinton and Bernie Sanders raised... *Combined!*[5]

You *can* make a difference. StressFreeBill is going to give you a specific strategy that can be extremely effective. Focus on the GOP primary races for the U.S. Senate and the U.S. Congress. The first thing you will want to do is identify who is running against the Ruling Class Politicians in the next primary election. If it helps, you can find StressFreeBill's opinions at www.PrimaryTheRulingClass.com.

The second thing is to set a budget for the current election cycle. Maybe a one-time contribution is all you're comfortable making or, perhaps, setting aside a small amount each month is within your capabilities. Don't take food off the table, but this is important – contribute accordingly.

Next, divide up your contribution amongst the GOP Ruling Class' opponents. This is important... Whether you are registered as Republican, Independent, Libertarian, or Democrat we must face the reality that a) Democrat primaries are rigged, and b) the Democrat party is imploding (sorry). If you want to be effective in combating the Ruling Class, we all need to focus our concentration on the Republican Party. This is not because you necessarily believe the Republican Party is better than the other parties; it is because this is the most effective way to break the back of the Ruling Class culture. Plain and simple – *to overcome the Ruling Class you will have to rise above party politics.*

For example, if you have budgeted a contribution of $100, instead of sending it to your favorite candidate divide it up into ten $10 contributions to ten different Ruling Class opponents. Do this whether you are their constituent (live in their districts) or not.

Lastly, challenge others to match your effort. Talk to your friends, use social media, etc. – do this to geometrically increase the power of your donation. Doubling your donation amount makes you a Player. Increasing it by a factor of five makes you a Star. Getting ten people to duplicate your efforts makes you a Superstar and you should be recognized. Send me an email through the StressFreeBill.com website and I'll try to figure out a way to reward you.

Information on how and when to donate to each candidate will be made available on PrimaryTheRulingClass.com.

Suggestion #6: For immediate change, focus on ousting Ruling Class Politicians. For long-term change, focus on reforming our educational system.

We need immediate change and this should be a focus for everyone. Your efforts to expose, identify, and defeat Ruling Class Politicians in primary elections is critically important. But we also need to address how we got into this mess in the first place...

We need to take back our educational system. We need to stop the ongoing socialist globalist indoctrination of our children. StressFreeBill is not some reactionary-alarmist crying wolf about this. Polls show that millennial's are more favorable to socialism than capitalism.[6] This would be all but impossible if our children were being given anything even close to an accurate depiction of world history. This trend *must* reverse itself or the United States will inevitably cease to be a free country.

The only way to accomplish this is for citizens to get involved in school boards. In most states, school board members are elected; in some states they are appointed.[7] [8] Whether it is by campaigning against Ruling Class school board members (Intelligentsia), entering the race to be elected yourself, or just attending the school board meetings to make your voice heard, this is an important way you can patriotically contribute. If you would like to coordinate locally or with others across the nation in this effort, feel free to post announcements in the comments section below the articles on the StressFreeBill.com website. We particularly recommend the article, *Taking Back Our Schools and Universities*. We will do our best to act as a clearinghouse.

Although the socialist indoctrination of our children might be more obvious in the university system, it must by need be addressed first in our primary and secondary schools. This is also the area where any taxpaying citizen can have a significant voice – whether a parent or not.

Most public universities are run by Boards of Regents. Each state may vary in how it operates, but working through the state government is the first part of a two-pronged approach. Demand accountability from your state legislators and Regents; face the issue head on and insist that socialistic indoctrination will not be tolerated. The second prong is to apply financial pressure to offending institutions. If a particular professor is espousing anti-American ideals, and especially if the administration is supporting him or her in it, go public. Call local radio and TV stations, write a blog, start a movement... Let parents know what they are sending their kids into when they enroll them at that school. Declining enrollments and declining donations are powerful motivators. Just ask the University of Missouri. Freshman enrollments dropped by over 2,000 students in the two years following the very public Black Lives Matter protests held there in 2015. The administration projects that it will need to lay off 400 faculty and administrators as a result. [9] [10]

The single best thing you can do, however, is to take the responsibility yourself to educate your children on American Exceptionalism. Talk about the value of capitalism, free speech, and private property rights. If your children are young there are any number of books out there written about patriotism and history – make a habit of reading to them every day (Rush Limbaugh authors an especially well written series). In StressFreeBill's family, we have a long held tradition at each holiday dinner to discuss what the holiday is about. On Christmas and Easter we talk about our faith, on Thanksgiving we talk about the Pilgrims and what we are thankful for, and on the Fourth of July we each read a section of the Declaration of Independence. Veterans Day and Memorial Day are especially poignant for us.

Create your own traditions, set your own standards... But make sure your children (and grandchildren) know that you don't think patriotism is passé. Let them know that you love your country with all your heart and chances are good they will too.

Suggestion #7: Consider supporting the Convention of States (COS) movement.

A little-known fact is that our Founding Fathers anticipated we might find ourselves in this situation - a situation where forces totally unresponsive to the will of the people have taken control of our federal government. This is why they included a special provision in Article V of the United States

Constitution. What follows, is the first part of that article:

Article V
The Congress, whenever two thirds of both houses shall deem it necessary, shall propose amendments to this Constitution, **or, on the application of the legislatures of two thirds of the several states**, shall call a convention for proposing amendments, which, in either case, shall be valid to all intents and purposes, as part of this Constitution... (Emphasis added)

Article V discusses how to amend the Constitution of the United States. Most people think this must be done by Congress and, indeed, it usually has been. However, the phrase in bold allows the states to take the matter into their own hands and totally bypass the U.S. Congress. This is done through the vehicle of calling a Convention of States.

Through my own unscientific survey I have asked hundreds of individuals if they felt like Term Limits would be a good idea for the United States Senate and House of Representatives. Almost everyone indicates it would be a great idea. When I then ask them if they think it will ever happen, however, they almost always say no – no one believes that politicians are going to vote term limits on themselves. The same can be said for trying to pass a balanced budget amendment – Congress derives its prestige and authority from the power of the purse. Few congressmen would vote to dramatically curtail their own power by putting a clamp on how much money can be spent.

There are a number of issues like this where Congress has gotten totally out of hand; there are many areas where the power of the federal government has overreached its original constitutional mandate. This needs to be addressed and it needs to be fixed. This is another area that would be worthy of an entire book and fortunately, there are a couple of good ones out there.[11] [12] You can find more of StressFreeBill's thoughts on this at the StressFreeBill.com website, but we would encourage you to support this movement with your voice, actions, and dollars. Some of the most brilliant minds in our country have created videos, seminars, and written books about this very real movement. Already a number of states have ratified their application. A good starting point to learn more would be their Facebook page at www.Facebook.com/ConventionOfStates (Convention Of States Project), or their website at: www.ConventionOfStates.com.

Suggestion #8: Show your patriotism every day in every way.

The United States is a force for good in this world. We are not perfect or even close to it, but we get it right more often than we get it wrong and there is no question that we have led the world in a direction that has benefited billions of people. We are guilty of great sins, but we have also corrected many of those sins and helped the rest of the world do the same. We have perpetrated our share of injustices, but when our public conscious becomes aware we inevitably rectify them.

We have sometimes been ruthless in protecting our interests, but we have been just as ruthless and spilt much of our own blood in defending the interests, property, and freedom of others...

So when you add up all of the pluses and minuses throughout our 240+ year history we are not a good country – we are a *great* country.

StressFreeBill will proudly stand for the national anthem and place his hand over his heart to say the Pledge of Allegiance. I will proudly wave my flag on the Fourth of July and display it at every opportunity. This is not out of naïveté; this is not the babble of some brainwashed idiot conforming to the indoctrination of his masters...

Napoleon Bonaparte once said, "A soldier will fight long and hard for a bit of colored ribbon." This was a rather cynical statement uttered by a man that was ruthless in his ambition and who used nationalism as a tool for manipulation. I'm sure there are Ruling Class Politicians here that look at American patriotism just as cynically. They, like Napoleon, confuse the government of the United States with the ideals of America.

The Ruling Class Intelligentsia will not recognize this distinction, and will go out of their way to teach your children that you are silly and naïve. Ruling Class Suck-ups in the entertainment industry will make fun of you, and the Ruling Class Media will spread that ridicule far and wide...

But what they cannot do is steal your resolve.

If you love our country and what it stands for, I beseech you... Show it every day in every way. Show it with your voice, show it in your confidence, and show it with your resolve.

Suggestion #9: If you are so inclined, ask God daily to bless the United States of America.

You may or may not believe in a higher power; there is certainly no requirement for this to join us in our efforts to oppose the self-appointed Ruling Class in America. However, if you do, I would ask you to remember our country in your prayers.

StressFreeBill nightly asks for God's blessing and guidance for our President and our country. Many times it's a very short prayer, other times it's more like this…

> God, thank you for the opportunity to live in the freest country on earth. Thank you for the abundance and riches you have granted us and the boundless opportunities available for our children. And especially thank you for the men and women who have gone before us and given so much to make these freedoms available to me and mine. God, give me the courage to do the same. Give me the strength of conviction to use my voice, energy, and vote to ensure those freedoms can be passed on to future generations. Grant me the wisdom to be effective in leadership, and protect me against the temptations to abuse it. Bless and guide our President and leaders, and God bless the United States of America. Thank you, Amen.

My prayers are almost always a private concern but I do make an exception around the children. At the dinner table, especially around the holidays, bowing our heads in prayer and thanks is a welcomed tradition. I think it important that our children grow up knowing that our country was founded on a belief that certain inalienable rights are given to men and women by our Creator. I think it important that our children grow up knowing that we still believe this. I think it important our children see us being thankful.

CHAPTER TWENTY-ONE

Final Thoughts

On the one hand, this book is full of revelations. On the other, there will be people that say, *"This is nothing new; Washington has always been this way."* Both viewpoints are somewhat correct...

In short, this book documents how a new Ruling Class culture has developed in our country. It exposes globalism as the uniting force behind the Ruling Class movement and details how this sense of elitism has all but taken over a number of critical professions. It validates that this has resulted in a very real movement towards socialism and explains how this movement became a pervasive *culture* under President Obama.

Washington DC has always been a swamp where oligarchs bribe politicians, intelligentsias espouse their theories and solicit sponsorships, and the media pursues its own ratings agenda. It has always held an element of corruption, below the table dealing, insider's knowledge, and a sense of elitism. The difference was that the underlying culture was always pro-American. We are now, however, long past the days of John F. Kennedy extolling American

Exceptionalism and declaring that *Americans* would walk on the moon...

As we have clearly demonstrated in this book, the new Ruling Class culture is now decidedly *anti-American*.

Those immersed in this culture would vociferously deny this, of course, but we have focused here on the study of *behavior* – not platitudes or excuses. The traditional American values of self-reliance, hard work for success, equality of opportunity not outcome, and even the rule of law are now considered passé. America is not viewed as an exceptional country; we are just a country like any other.

StressFreeBill believes the key insight this book has to offer is an understanding that this new self-appointed Ruling Class is a culture in and of itself. It is this *culture* that provides the coordination between the disconnected and disparate professions. It is this culture that justifies the unethical, anti-American, and many times illegal behavior. It is this culture that sustains the feedback bubble that cocoons and reinforces its members in their arrogant beliefs.

It is frustrating to watch show hosts, news anchors, pundits and politicians act incredulous when a Republican Congress doesn't pass promised legislation. They shake their heads and ask each other how this can possibly be? We watch these same people ask why Congressional and Senate leadership doesn't do something?

This book provides what should be an obvious answer; they don't want to. More specifically, this book explains *why* they don't want to – and that's really been the missing piece to allow understanding and acceptance.

No one wants to believe that their leaders are disingenuous. No one wants to believe that their elected officials have sold them out and now answer to a 'higher' power. No one wants to believe that patriotism is dead. No one wants to accept that forces we cannot control have decided to throw our futures onto a path not of our choosing…

And we don't have to.

This book also outlines suggestions on how *We the People* can take our country *and our culture* back. StressFreeBill is a professional writer and has hopes to profit from this book, but please believe me when I say; *this is a work of love.*

This is about love for our country. It's about appreciation for all the members of my family that served and spilled blood protecting our freedoms. It's about the future; that utopian glimpse of what things *could* look like given to a small boy watching the TV show Star Trek. It's about traveling the world and seeing firsthand the poverty and misery created when American values aren't present. And it's about the incredible awe I hold for our Founding Fathers and what I believe was their divinely inspired vision.

Writing this book is *the least* I can do to contribute to the fight against our new self-appointed Ruling Class. I hope you will find your own way to contribute and I welcome you to the cause.

StressFreeBill

Please Help Spread the Word...

If you Enjoyed Reading
It's Not About
Donkeys and Elephants
Please Tell Others About it

An Easy to Share Article About This Book
Can be Found at:
www.StressFreeBill.com/Spread-The-Word
Fill Free to Share it on Social Media
(Just click on the article's social media icons)

Also, stay up to date on current events
and how the Ruling Class is influencing them...
Register to receive email notification of
StressFreeBill's newest blog posts.
www.StressFreeBill.com

If you enjoy reading Science fiction
Check out this author's books at:
www.WilliamLeeGordon.com

About The Author
www.StressFreeBill.com
www.PrimaryTheRulingClass.com

StressFreeBill is a moniker that was bestowed on Bill a number of years ago when social media sites were getting started.

To this day he has a large online following because of his many businesses, careers, and vocations.

He left college to start his first business, a regional fast-food franchise (he was the sweat-equity partner).

From there he went on to sales and sales management. Always as an Independent Contractor he sold everything from Wholesale Junior Fashion Clothing to insurance – and ended up building the third largest region in the country for a national health insurance company.

Attracted to the healthcare industry, he later started a number of different businesses under both traditional and direct-selling models. He actually built, and for over a decade maintained, a 30,000+ member international direct selling organization.

He is a public speaker and now a best-selling author.

Throughout his adult life he has always been self-employed or a business owner – he has never been an employee.

He has experienced incredible success and suffered terrible failure. He believes in hard work, never quitting, and didn't let growing up without a father in a poor household hold him back.

Bill has always loved to live the present and dream the future. Like many authors, he draws from his real-life experiences for his inspiration. In what he still considers to be the first half of his adult life, he has (among other things):

- Performed with and taken improvisation lessons from one of the greatest Jazz trumpet performers of all time, Clark Terry.
- Scored a touchdown in a football game.
- Been elected to the Student Government of his university as well as president of his fraternity *and* the Interfraternity Council.
- Taught Lifesaving Swimming classes for the Red Cross.
- Hiked the rainforest, walked the Copacabana, and whitewater rafted in the mountains above Rio de Janeiro.
- He has actually read the Bible, the Constitution of the United States, and the Declaration of Independence.
- He has stood alone at the summit, preparing to be the last skier off the mountain, watching a blizzard blow in across the Rockies.
- He has received standing ovations from thousands of listeners for speeches given across four continents spanning three decades.
- He has witnessed unbelievable abject poverty, and dined at some of the most renowned restaurants in the world.
- He has been a pallbearer... and been named a godfather.
- He has driven in a Demolition Derby.

- He has cruised the Caribbean and scuba-dived some of the most beautiful locations in the world.
- He has witnessed what is considered to be the most beautiful sunrise in the world from the 10,000 ft. rim of the Haleakala volcano in Maui, Hawaii.
- He helped support an orphanage in Honduras.
- He has hot air ballooned, and picnicked in remote locations only accessible by helicopter.
- He has learned another language.
- He has travelled the high-speed trains of Europe and gazed, open-mouthed, at some of the most amazing frescoes and architecture.
- He has owned a tuxedo.
- He earned and by tradition claimed the just finished crystal decanter of Louis XIII cognac from the Ritz Carlton in Sarasota, FL.
- He met his future wife while traveling on another continent and returned there many times to court her.
- He has eaten lunch atop the Schilthorn Mountain in the Swiss Alps and stayed at the Grand Victoria-Jungfrau, a palace built for Queen Victoria in 1856.
- He has piloted a small plane.
- He has stood side-by-side with the governor of Guam, bracing against the ever-blowing winds, standing on the steps of the Congress Building, overlooking paradise.

- He has raced a NASCAR, and stayed at the hotel made famous by the Eagles in their song, Hotel California.
- He once took 5th Place in a National Foosball Championship tournament.
- He was married in a third-world country, on another continent, in another language, and in a church whose immense beauty was in its poverty and austerity.
- He has now written multiple novels and sold tens of thousands of copies across five continents.

He hopes this list pales in comparison to what he does in the future…

REFERENCES

Chapter Two References - You Can't Win the Fight If You Can't Even Name Your Enemy...

[1] http://www.frontpagemag.com/fpm/265678/berkeley-riots-provoked-freedom-center-campaign-matthew-vadum

[2] https://en.wikipedia.org/wiki/List_of_Republicans_who_opposed_the_Donald_Trump_presidential_campaign,_2016

[3] http://observer.com/2016/07/wikileaks-proves-primary-was-rigged-dnc-undermined-democracy/

[4] http://www.gallup.com/poll/201974/congress-job-approval-start-new-session.aspx

[5] https://www.opensecrets.org/overview/reelect.php

[6] http://www.businessinsider.com/byrd-rule-obamacare-replacement-trumpcare-senate-2017-3

[7] http://www.slate.com/blogs/moneybox/2017/04/25/donald_trump_s_corporate_tax_cuts_can_t_pass_congress.html

[8] http://freebeacon.com/politics/stephanopoulos-does-not-disclose-clinton-connections-hillary-town-hall/

[9] https://www.usatoday.com/story/opinion/2015/05/16/stephanopoulos-abc-clinton-schweizer-foundation-hillary-column/27436475/

[10] http://www.breitbart.com/2016-presidential-race/2016/11/06/george-stephanopoulos-wife-leaving-trump-wins/

[11] http://www.pickensprogressonline.com/2015/editorials/staff-written-edits/4290-political-nastiness-also-an-american-tradition

12   https://www.merriam-webster.com/words-at-play/are-presidential-campaigns-getting-nastier-not-really/hermaphroditical

13   http://www.washingtonexaminer.com/media-move-to-delegitimize-trumps-victory/article/2609890

14 http://www.history.com/topics/vietnam-war/ho-chi-minh

15 https://en.wikipedia.org/wiki/Karl_Marx

16 http://www.economist.com/blogs/economist-explains/2015/07/economist-explains-20

17   http://www.breitbart.com/big-government/2015/12/13/climate-change-deal-is-a-threat-to-u-s-sovereignty/

18   https://www.reference.com/government-politics/examples-inalienable-rights-320a79f3523bcdd5#

Chapter Three References - It's Not About Issues - It's About Freedom

1 https://www.dailydot.com/layer8/voter-turnout-2016/

2   http://observer.com/2016/07/wikileaks-proves-primary-was-rigged-dnc-undermined-democracy/

3 https://www.cliffsnotes.com/literature/r/republic/about-platos-republic

4 http://www.heritage.org/government-regulation/commentary/government-the-people-or-over-the-people

5   http://www.breitbart.com/big-government/2017/02/24/steve-bannon-nailed-it-on-the-medias-fight-against-trump/

6 http://nypost.com/2016/11/11/new-york-times-we-blew-it-on-trump/

7   http://www.breitbart.com/2016-presidential-race/2016/12/09/intercept-clinton-fan-manufactured-fake-news-msnbc-personalities-spread-discredit-wikileaks-docs/

8 http://mediashift.org/2014/10/advocacy-is-not-a-dirty-word-in-journalism/

9
https://www.google.com/url?sa=t&rct=j&q=&esrc=s&source=web&cd=4&cad=rja&uact
=8&ved=0ahUKEwi0gY-
v65rVAhWe14MKHbhBD_gQFgg_MAM&url=https%3A%2F%2Fwww.vox.com%2Fp
olicy-and-politics%2F2017%2F5%2F22%2F15629974%2Fsenate-byrd-rule-obamacare-
repeal&usg=AFQjCNE8O1_GBLY_jA-HkmmzVSmaVwlSog

10   http://www.washingtonexaminer.com/rick-perry-anti-trump-leakers-should-leave-the-government/article/2623584

[11]   http://www.cnbc.com/2017/05/25/uk-stops-sharing-intelligence-with-us-following-manchester-attack.html

[12] http://study.com/academy/lesson/judicial-activism-vs-judicial-restraint.html

[13]   http://www.desmoinesregister.com/story/opinion/letters/2017/02/25/out-control-judiciary-marks-real-threat-letter/98155332/

[14] http://www.foxnews.com/politics/2017/05/25/trump-travel-ban-blocked-by-va-based-federal-appeals-court.html?cmpid=googextension

[15] http://www.discoverthenetworks.org/viewSubCategory.asp?id=1237

[16]
https://www.forbes.com/forbes/welcome/?toURL=https://www.forbes.com/sites/kathleen chaykowski/2017/02/21/mark-zuckerberg-is-running-a-political-campaign-just-not-for-elected-office/&refURL=https://www.forbes.com/forbes/welcome/?toURL=https://www.forbes.com/sites/kathleenchaykowski/2017/02/21/mark-zuckerberg-is-running-a-political-campaign-just-not-for-elected-office/&refURL=https://www.google.com/&referrer=https://www.google.com/&referrer=https://www.forbes.com/forbes/welcome/?toURL=https://www.forbes.com/sites/kathleenchaykowski/2017/02/21/mark-zuckerberg-is-running-a-political-campaign-just-not-for-elected-office/&refURL=https://www.google.com/&referrer=https://www.google.com/

Chapter Four References - Understanding that Government Is Not Our Friend

[1] http://www.heritage.org/political-process/commentary/the-american-experiment

[2] http://www.dispatch.com/opinion/20170320/letter-federal-government-is-our-friend

[3] http://www.grisanik.com/blog/government-is-our-friend/

[4]   https://nccs.net/online-resources/our-ageless-constitution/the-unique-idea-of-the-american-constitution

[5] https://www.billofrightsinstitute.org/founding-documents/bill-of-rights/

Chapter Five References - The Ruling Class Media

[1] http://www.theamericanmirror.com/cnn-host-calls-trump-piece-sht-renewed-call-travel-ban/

[2] http://www.mediaite.com/online/nbc-news-throws-shade-on-president-trumps-terror-tweet-info-is-unconfirmed/

3   https://www.forbes.com/sites/katevinton/2016/06/01/these-15-billionaires-own-americas-news-media-companies/#28cbbd07660a

Chapter Six References - The Ruling Class Intelligentsia

1 https://en.wikipedia.org/wiki/Intelligentsia

2 https://plato.stanford.edu/entries/moral-relativism/

3 https://plato.stanford.edu/entries/identity-politics/

4   http://www.zerohedge.com/news/2017-01-27/barack-obama-now-only-president-history-never-have-year-3-gdp-growth

5   http://www.aei.org/publication/team-obama-sorry-america-the-new-normal-may-be-here-to-stay/

6 http://thehill.com/blogs/pundits-blog/the-administration/310103-a-tale-of-two-cabinets-obamas-cronies-vs-trumps

Chapter Seven References - Ruling Class Politicians

1 http://eyler.freeservers.com/JeffPers/jefpco33.htm

2 https://www.dailydot.com/layer8/voter-turnout-2016/

3   http://www.businessinsider.com/these-6-corporations-control-90-of-the-media-in-america-2012-6

4   http://www.breitbart.com/2016-presidential-race/2016/10/18/revealed-96-percent-of-medias-campaign-donations-went-to-clinton/

5 http://www.twc.edu/twcnow/blogs/student/9072/washington-bubble

Chapter Eight References - How Congress Gets Away With Lying To Us

1   https://www.washingtonpost.com/news/the-fix/wp/2017/03/09/the-budget-rule-youve-never-heard-of-that-ties-republicans-hands-on-obamacare/?utm_term=.7521fd8f95e5

2   https://www.vox.com/policy-and-politics/2017/5/2/15515834/filibuster-kill-abolish-nuclear-option-trump-mcconnell

[3] https://en.wikipedia.org/wiki/Reconciliation_(United_States_Congress)

[4] http://www.politico.com/story/2013/11/harry-reid-nuclear-option-100199

[5]   https://www.nytimes.com/2017/04/06/us/politics/neil-gorsuch-supreme-court-senate.html

[6]   http://www.politifact.com/truth-o-meter/statements/2013/nov/22/harry-reid/harry-reid-among-flip-floppers-senates-nuclear-opt/

[7]   http://www.wsj.com/livecoverage/house-republican-health-care-obamacare-replacement-bill-vote

Chapter Nine References - Ruling Class Oligarchs

[1] https://en.wikipedia.org/wiki/Mark_Zuckerberg

[2] https://en.wikipedia.org/wiki/K_Street_(Washington,_D.C.)

[3]   http://www.businessinsider.com/these-6-corporations-control-90-of-the-media-in-america-2012-6

[4]   https://www.forbes.com/sites/katevinton/2016/06/01/these-15-billionaires-own-americas-news-media-companies/#28cbbd07660a

[5]   http://www.independent.co.uk/news/world/americas/koch-brothers-donald-trump-clash-resistance-conservative-billionaires-network-us-president-charles-a7560706.html

[6] http://www.discoverthenetworks.org/viewSubCategory.asp?id=1237

[7]   http://www.thegatewaypundit.com/2016/11/soros-funded-orgs-behind-violent-anti-trump-protests-across-america/

Chapter Ten References - Who Is George Soros?

[1] https://www.georgesoros.com/books/the_age_of_failability/

[2] http://humanevents.com/2011/04/02/top-10-reasons-george-soros-is-dangerous/

[3]https://books.google.com/books?id=FY5J-9hy2fMC&pg=PR29&lpg=PR29&dq=%E2%80%9CInsofar+as+there+are+collective+interests+that+transcend+state+boundaries,+the+sovereignty+of+states+must+be+subordinated+to+international+law+and+international+institutions.%E2%80%9D&source=bl&ots=aPi7ztOaVb&sig=nl0570IwUVEKGNULyrVCCpOcOBY&hl=en&sa=X&ved=0ahUKEwjikfa4kN_UAhXFy4MKHUNwAgcQ6AEISTAF#v=onepage&q=%E2%80%9CInsofar%20as%20there%20are%20collective%20interests%20that%20transcend%20state%20boundaries%2C%20the%20sovereignty%20of%20states%20must%20be%20subordinated%20to%20international%20law%20and%20international%20institutions.%E2%80%9D&f=true

[4] http://www.westernjournalism.com/koch-brothers-george-soros-fear/

[5] All the organizations listed, except when cited separately, carry the following citation: http://www.discoverthenetworks.org/viewSubCategory.asp?id=1237

[6] http://www.washingtontimes.com/news/2016/aug/16/black-lives-matter-cashes-100-million-liberal-foun/

[7] http://www.reuters.com/article/us-wallstreet-protests-origins-idUSTRE79C1YN20111014

[8] http://www.washingtontimes.com/news/2015/jan/14/george-soros-funds-ferguson-protests-hopes-to-spur/

[9] http://www.insidesources.com/standing-rock-protests-tied-soros-funded-group/

[10] http://www.activistpost.com/2016/11/looks-like-george-soros-funding-trump-protests-just-like-funded-ferguson-riots.html

[11] http://www.lifezette.com/polizette/soros-fingerprints-notmypresident-protests/

[12] http://www.washingtontimes.com/news/2017/mar/7/george-soros-gave-246-million-partners-womens-marc/

[13] http://www.investors.com/politics/editorials/george-soros-the-hillary-democrats-billionaire-puppetmaster/

[14] http://thehill.com/blogs/pundits-blog/presidential-campaign/300992-hillary-soros-and-the-political-genocide-of

[15] http://humanevents.com/2006/04/07/emexclusive-emthe-truth-about-la-raza/

[16] http://www.breitbart.com/milo/2017/02/05/refuse-fascism-group-behind-berkeley-riot-funded-george-soros/

[17] http://www.breitbart.com/big-government/2016/12/09/activist-served-george-soros-financed-boards-behind-scheme-usurp-trumps-electoral-college-votes/

[18] http://www.breitbart.com/big-journalism/2016/12/16/soros-finances-group-helping-facebook-flag-disputed-stories/

[19] http://www.breitbart.com/big-government/2017/01/28/george-soros-financed-groups-scheme-stop-trumps-temporary-refugee-halt-order/

[20] http://www.lifezette.com/polizette/soros-fingerprints-all-over-anti-trump-lawsuits/

[21] http://www.breitbart.com/big-government/2017/02/19/obamas-organizing-action-partners-soros-linked-indivisible-disrupt-trumps-agenda/

[22] http://www.breitbart.com/big-government/2017/02/06/records-soros-fund-execs-funded-paul-ryan-marco-rubio-jeb-bush-john-mccain-john-kasich-lindsey-graham-in-2016/

²³ https://www.insidephilanthropy.com/home/2015/9/14/philanthropy-vs-tyranny-inside-the-open-society-foundations.html

Chapter Eleven References - Ruling Class Judiciary

¹ https://www.edu.gov.mb.ca/k12/cur/socstud/foundation_gr8/blms/8-3-5e.pdf

² http://www.washingtontimes.com/news/2016/sep/12/founders-intended-tension-in-co-equal-branches/

Chapter Twelve References - The Ruling Class Bureaucracy

¹   https://theintercept.com/2017/02/14/the-leakers-who-exposed-gen-flynns-lie-committed-serious-and-wholly-justified-felonies/

²   http://www.foxnews.com/politics/2017/03/20/comey-says-leaks-could-constitute-espionage.html

³   http://www.cnsnews.com/news/article/terence-p-jeffrey/21955000-12329000-government-employees-outnumber-manufacturing

⁴   http://www.thegatewaypundit.com/2016/05/obamas-america-us-government-now-nearly-many-employees-fortune-500-companies-combined/

⁵ https://en.wikipedia.org/wiki/United_States_federal_civil_service

⁶ http://presidentialtransition.org/blog/posts/160316_help-wanted-4000-appointees.php

⁷   https://www.washingtonpost.com/graphics/politics/trump-transition-appointments-scale/

⁸ http://www.bbc.com/news/world-us-canada-38726982

⁹   http://www.politifact.com/truth-o-meter/statements/2017/jan/24/sean-spicer/sean-spicers-claim-federal-workforce-has-expanded-/

¹⁰ http://www.nationalreview.com/article/445230/federal-government-growth-continues-while-federal-employee-numbers-hold

¹¹   http://www.washingtontimes.com/news/2017/jan/17/john-brennan-wants-legacy-be-work-he-did-lgbtq-com/

¹²   http://dailycaller.com/2017/01/17/outgoing-cia-director-known-for-wearing-rainbow-lanyard-at-office-to-show-lgbt-solidarity/

¹³ https://spectator.org/leaky-john-brennan/

[14]   http://www.freedomworks.org/content/chuck-schumers-unprecedented-unreasonable-demand-slow-walk-trumps-cabinet-nominees

[15]   http://www.washingtontimes.com/news/2017/jan/19/senate-democrats-vow-delays-on-votes-for-trumps-ca/

[16] https://www.washingtonpost.com/graphics/politics/how-long-confirmations-will-take/

[17]   http://dailysignal.com/2016/12/08/obama-political-employees-to-continue-as-career-employees-under-trump/

[18]   http://www.washingtontimes.com/news/2016/nov/27/obama-appointees-burrowing-in-for-career-federal-j/

[19]   http://hotair.com/archives/2015/03/02/cbs-just-how-hard-is-it-to-fire-a-federal-govt-employee/

[20] http://dailycaller.com/2016/03/03/heres-why-its-all-but-impossible-to-fire-a-fed/

Chapter Fourteen References - Socialism vs Capitalism

[1]

https://simple.wikipedia.org/wiki/From_each_according_to_his_ability,_to_each_according_to_his_need

[2] https://fee.org/articles/why-communism-failed/

[3] https://en.wikipedia.org/wiki/The_Coming_China_Wars

[4] https://fee.org/articles/why-communism-failed/

[5] https://en.wikipedia.org/wiki/FairTax

[6] https://en.wikipedia.org/wiki/A_rising_tide_lifts_all_boats

[7]   http://www.telegraph.co.uk/travel/maps-and-graphics/most-generous-countries-in-the-world/

[8]   https://www.forbes.com/2008/12/24/america-philanthropy-income-oped-cx_ee_1226eaves.html#

[9] https://fee.org/articles/how-socialism-affects-charity/

[10] https://en.wikipedia.org/wiki/United_States_Constitution_and_worldwide_influence

Chapter Fifteen References - Climate Change

[1] http://thehill.com/media/306721-rasmussen-calls-itself-most-accurate-pollster-of-2016

[2] https://www.wsj.com/articles/cmo-today-media-stunned-by-trumps-win-1478695214

[3]   http://dailycaller.com/2015/12/28/climate-models-have-been-wrong-about-global-warming-for-six-decades/

[4] https://climatesight.org/2012/01/20/how-do-climate-models-work/

[5]   http://www.washingtontimes.com/news/2017/feb/5/climate-change-whistleblower-alleges-noaa-manipula/

[6] https://www.scientificamerican.com/article/sun-spots-and-climate-change/

[7] http://sciencing.com/sunspots-affect-climate-4567096.html

[8]   http://www.climatedepot.com/2015/11/04/no-global-warming-at-all-for-18-years-9-months-a-new-record-the-pause-lengthens-again-just-in-time-for-un-summit-in-paris/

[9]   http://www.breitbart.com/big-government/2017/06/20/delingpole-the-pause-in-global-warming-is-real-admits-climategate-scientist/

[10] http://www.history.com/this-day-in-history/galileo-is-convicted-of-heresy

[11] https://www.wired.com/2012/06/famous-persecuted-scientists/

[12] http://dailycaller.com/2013/08/29/mit-professor-global-warming-is-a-religion/

[13]   http://www.breitbart.com/radio/2017/06/01/bolton-paris-climate-accord-objective-reduction-national-sovereignty-global-governance/

[14]
http://www.climatefocus.com/sites/default/files/20151228%20COP%2021%20briefing%20FIN.pdf

Chapter Sixteen References - Globalism vs Nationalism

[1] https://bea.gov/papers/pdf/HMS1.PDF

[2] https://en.wikipedia.org/wiki/Effects_of_NAFTA_on_Mexico

[3] http://www.epi.org/blog/naftas-impact-workers/

[4]   https://www.washingtonpost.com/news/wonk/wp/2016/05/11/the-middle-class-is-shrinking-just-about-everywhere-in-america/?utm_term=.7e981e63d7d8

[5]   http://constructionlitmag.com/politics/international/the-rise-of-the-multinational-corporation/

6
https://www.realclearpolitics.com/video/2015/06/22/jeff_sessions_trade_agreements_ced e_us_sovereignty_permanently_to_new_transnational_authority_same_language_used_to _start_the_european_union.html

7   https://www.citizen.org/our-work/globalization-and-trade/more-power-corporations-attack-nations

8   http://www.vir.com.vn/foreign-textile-firms-reel-out-new-investments-in-anticipation-of-tpp.html

9   https://www.cato.org/blog/withdrawing-tpp-was-senseless-act-wanton-destruction?gclid=CjwKEAjws-LKBRDCk9v6_cnBgjISJAADkzXefNAw9w1neXBteXiWoXwhlh66M_Ba2svvgHW21s srCRoCErTw_wcB

10 https://www.thetrumpet.com/2061-the-death-of-american-manufacturing

11   http://www.businessinsider.com/labor-force-participation-rate-falls-to-38-year-low-2015-7

12   https://blow.blogs.nytimes.com/2008/07/31/they-have-more-honors-kids-than-we-have-kids/

13   http://www.dailymail.co.uk/news/article-4037392/Disney-fired-250-American-workers-replaced-Indian-staff-visas-suit-says.html

14   http://www.huffingtonpost.com/judy-frankel/insourcing-american-lose-_b_11173074.html

15   https://www.usnews.com/news/articles/2016-05-17/more-stem-degrees-going-to-foreign-students

16 http://www.businessinsider.com/stem-majors-earn-a-lot-more-money-after-graduation-2014-7

17 https://www.usnews.com/news/slideshows/5-countries-that-take-the-most-immigrants

18 https://en.wikipedia.org/wiki/American_exceptionalism

19 https://www.youtube.com/watch?v=c32G868tor0&feature=youtu.be

Chapter Seventeen References - Making Sense of it All

1 https://www.mercatus.org/publication/spending-under-president-george-w-bush

2 https://en.wikipedia.org/wiki/It%27s_the_economy,_stupid

3 http://www.huffingtonpost.ca/2013/12/29/nafta-mexico_n_4515862.html

[4] http://money.cnn.com/2017/01/25/news/economy/mexico-remittances-trump/index.html

[5] http://www.businessinsider.com/the-sinaloa-cartel-and-colombian-cocaine-2015-8

[6] http://www.mysanantonio.com/news/local/article/Reynosa-journalists-navigate-dangers-to-cover-11148290.php

[7] http://www.breitbart.com/texas/2015/04/18/us-state-department-181-americans-murdered-in-mexico-since-2013/

[8] http://www.businessinsider.com/tech-company-donations-clinton-vs-trump-chart-2016-11

[9] http://www.politicalextortion.com/

[10] http://www.marketwatch.com/story/here-are-americas-biggest-corporate-donors-to-republicans-and-democrats-2015-10-27

[11] https://www.bloomberg.com/politics/graphics/2016-presidential-campaign-fundraising/july/public/index.html

[12] https://www.cato.org/publications/commentary/republicans-become-party-big-government

[13] http://www.americanpatriotdaily.com/latest/republicans-just-surrendered-to-obama-in-this-key-fight/

[14] http://www.politico.com/magazine/story/2015/12/ted-cruz-spending-gop-surrendering-to-obama-213448

Chapter Eighteen References - And Along Came Donald J. Trump

[1] https://en.wikipedia.org/wiki/New_world_order_(politics)

[2] http://swampland.time.com/2012/05/17/yes-washington-d-c-really-is-a-bubble/

[3] https://en.wikipedia.org/wiki/Republic_(Plato)

[4] http://time.com/3923128/donald-trump-announcement-speech/

[5] https://www.youtube.com/watch?v=5aYFC_7ZIn4&feature=youtu.be

[6] http://www.theblaze.com/news/2016/10/24/glenn-beck-explains-why-he-thinks-donald-trump-is-a-sociopath/

[7] https://www.washingtonpost.com/news/post-politics/wp/2016/01/23/glenn-beck-endorses-ted-cruz/?utm_term=.41f25d03975a

8

https://en.wikipedia.org/wiki/List_of_Republicans_who_opposed_the_Donald_Trump_pr
esidential_campaign,_2016

9 http://thehill.com/blogs/ballot-box/presidential-races/278141-republicans-who-vow-to-
never-back-trump

10 http://observer.com/2016/07/wikileaks-proves-primary-was-rigged-dnc-undermined-
democracy/

11

https://en.wikipedia.org/wiki/List_of_Republicans_who_opposed_the_Donald_Trump_pr
esidential_campaign,_2016

12 http://www.washingtonexaminer.com/louie-gohmert-house-gop-left-trump-to-dangle-
by-not-working-friday/article/2625456

Chapter Nineteen References - How It All Fits Together

1 http://www.breitbart.com/2016-presidential-race/2016/10/18/revealed-96-percent-of-
medias-campaign-donations-went-to-clinton/

2 https://www.usatoday.com/story/news/politics/2016/05/25/lawmaker-dues-party-
extortion-team-effort/84819738/

3 https://www.reviewjournal.com/news/politics-and-government/white-house-blames-
democrats-for-holding-up-trumps-nominees/

4 https://www.whitehouse.gov/the-press-office/2017/07/10/obstruction-alert-senate-
democrats-hold-blue-slips-delay-trumps-federal

5 http://www.nationalreview.com/article/430153/fast-furious-obama-first-scandal

6 https://www.forbes.com/sites/kellyphillipserb/2016/06/24/irs-targeting-scandal-citizens-
united-lois-lerner-and-the-20m-tax-saga-that-wont-go-away/#3204fe2dbcd1

7 http://www.clintoncashbook.com/

8 https://www.forbes.com/sites/frankminiter/2016/08/24/the-federal-government-is-
trying-to-grab-140-square-miles-of-private-land-in-texas/#3bca02f95694

9 http://dailysignal.com/2017/04/26/federal-land-grabs-have-gotten-out-of-control-why-
trumps-executive-order-is-a-positive-sign/

10 http://www.wpri.org/WPRI/Commentary/The-one-size-fits-all-federalization-of-local-
police-departments.htm

11 https://www.forbes.com/sites/paulroderickgregory/2017/01/13/the-trump-dossier-is-
false-news-and-heres-why/#6714e0368674

[12]   http://www.washingtonexaminer.com/james-comey-admits-leaking-his-trump-memo-to-the-press/article/2625346

[13]   https://www.circa.com/story/2017/05/23/politics/obama-intel-agency-secretly-conducted-illegal-searches-on-americans-for-years

[14]   http://www.foxnews.com/politics/2017/05/25/obama-s-nsa-rebuked-for-snooping-on-americans-journo-says-it-proves-wide-pattern.html

[15] http://heavy.com/news/2017/05/andrew-mccabe-interim-fbi-director-democrat-clinton-mcauliffe-politics-photos-bio-wife/

[16] https://www.quora.com/What-alleged-crimes-was-Hillary-Clinton-accused-of

[17] http://www.foxnews.com/politics/2017/04/03/soros-tied-networks-foundations-joined-forces-to-create-trump-resistance-fund.html

[18]   https://www.forbes.com/sites/paulroderickgregory/2017/01/13/the-trump-dossier-is-false-news-and-heres-why/#6714e0368674

[19]   http://projectveritas.com/2017/06/28/van-jones-russia-is-nothing-burger-american-pravda-cnn-part-ii/

[20]   https://www.forbes.com/sites/paulroderickgregory/2017/01/13/the-trump-dossier-is-false-news-and-heres-why/#714bd0b68674

[21] http://reason.com/blog/2017/07/16/mccain-and-the-trump-russia-dossier

[22]   http://www.cnn.com/2017/04/18/politics/fbi-dossier-carter-page-donald-trump-russia-investigation/index.html

[23]   http://thehill.com/policy/national-security/313555-comey-fbi-did-request-access-to-hacked-dnc-servers

[24] http://dailycaller.com/2017/06/24/crowdstrike-five-things-everyone-is-ignoring-about-the-russia-dnc-story/

[25]
http://www.slate.com/blogs/future_tense/2017/05/09/the_fbi_is_harder_to_trust_on_the_dnc_hack_because_it_relied_on_crowdstrike.html

[26]   http://www.washingtonexaminer.com/a-rather-large-new-york-times-correction/article/2627527

[27] http://heavy.com/news/2017/06/all-17-intelligence-agencies-did-not-say-russia-hacked-election-dnc-nyt-new-york-times/

[28] https://www.cnbc.com/2016/07/27/trump-hope-russia-finds-the-30000-emails-that-are-missing.html

[29]   http://thehill.com/blogs/ballot-box/presidential-races/289451-gingrich-trump-joking-on-russia-clinton-emails

[30] https://www.amazon.com/Shattered-Inside-Hillary-Clintons-Campaign/dp/0553447084

Chapter Twenty References - How to Make a Difference

[1]   http://www.journalism.org/2016/07/07/the-modern-news-consumer/pj_2016-07-07_modern-news-consumer_2-01/

[2]   http://wjla.com/news/nation-world/main-stream-media-continue-to-lose-the-publics-trust

[3]   http://www.washingtontimes.com/news/2017/apr/13/ed-gillespie-cory-stewart-frank-wagner-tangle-virg/

[4] http://www.cnn.com/2017/06/13/politics/virginia-governor-primary-results/index.html

[5]   http://www.washingtontimes.com/news/2017/feb/21/trump-smashes-obamas-small-donor-fundraising-pace/

[6]   https://www.washingtonpost.com/news/rampage/wp/2016/02/05/millennials-have-a-higher-opinion-of-socialism-than-of-capitalism/?utm_term=.9e78c1470abd

[7] https://www.nsba.org/sites/default/files/reports/electionschart.pdf

[8] https://www.nsba.org/about-us/frequently-asked-questions

[9]   http://dailycaller.com/2017/05/08/mizzous-enrollment-has-plummeted-since-it-got-woke/

[10]   http://www.stltoday.com/news/local/education/declining-enrollment-adds-to-budget-woes-at-the-university-of/article_3a1afcdd-b22d-50c1-8848-df0e15196f38.html

[11]
https://www.conventionofstates.com/tom_coburn_s_new_book_article_v_bypass_a_corrupt_congress

[12]   https://www.amazon.com/dp/B00CO4IP5M/ref=dp-kindle-redirect?_encoding=UTF8&btkr=1